You Must have a Dream to have a Dream Come True!

Ann's Blueprint for Success Through Goal-Setting and Perseverance

Ann McNeill

THE MASTER BUILDER

Copyright © 2025

Ann Mcneill
The Master Builder

You Must have a Dream to have a
Dream Come True!

ISBN#: 979-8-88526-712-0

First Printing
July 2025

McNeill, Ann

Printed in the U.S.A.

Foreword

by
Les Brown,
Nationally Renowned Motivational Speaker

It is a profound honor and pleasure to write the foreword for "You Must Have a Dream," authored by my dear friend of over 40 years, Ann McNeill. Our journey together began in the 1970s, when we were both young, ambitious, and driven by an insatiable hunger for success. Ann McNeill has helped shape me into the man I am today. Her influence, guidance, and unwavering belief in the power of dreams have left an indelible mark on my life.

Over the decades, I have watched Ann transform not only her life but the lives of countless others through her unwavering commitment to goal-setting and strategic planning. Ann's life is a testament to the principles outlined in Napoleon Hill's, Think and Grow Rich. She has lived and breathed these principles, becoming the poster child for what focused, disciplined, and balanced living can achieve. Ann's incredible achievements in the construction industry, a field historically dominated by men and with very few Black women, are a reflection of her courage, integrity, and relentless determination. Her pioneering spirit led her to establish McNeill Construction (MCO) and the National Association of Black Women in Construction, both of which have become pillars of excellence and empowerment.

In You Must Have a Dream, Ann generously shares the secrets to her success, providing a comprehensive guide to setting and achieving goals across ten crucial categories: spirituality, family, finances, education, health, business, personal development, civics, recreation, and creativity. What makes this book truly special is Ann's willingness to share her personal experiences and the challenges she has faced. Through her stories, readers will find a relatable, authentic voice that demonstrates how perseverance, focus, and self-discipline can lead to extraordinary accomplishments.

Ann has always exemplified class and integrity, facing life's vicissitudes with grace and resilience. Her success is not only a personal triumph but a beacon of hope and inspiration for others who dare to dream big.

This book is not just a guide; it is a testament to the power of dreams and the transformative impact of strategic planning and goal-setting. Ann's story is a beacon of light for all who seek to live a life of purpose, balance, and success. It is with great pride and admiration that I introduce you to 'You Must Have a Dream, by Ann McNeill.

Les Brown

Dedication

This book and the concomitant workbook is dedicated to my late dad, L.C. Cobb, who taught me the value of hard work by example, instilling in me the principle to work as if everything depended on me. To my late mother, Alberta Cobb, who showed me the power of prayer, teaching me to pray as if everything depended on God.

To my husband, Daniel McNeill, my boyfriend since 1974, thank you for the countless opportunities for growth in every area of my life. In your own way, you are my biggest supporter and number one fan. Through your example, I have learned that a life centered around family values, next to my salvation, is more important than all dreams and achievements.

Every achievement is a team effort, and this book would not be possible without the support and guidance of my friend since 1994, Dr. Mia Y. Merritt. Your incredible patience, encouragement, and relentless push for me to write have been invaluable. Thank you for helping me to bring this book out of my heart and into my hands. I thank my children and grandchildren, for family is the joy that resonates in my heart. They are my pride, my joy, and my gifts from God.

I also extend my gratitude to every masterminder who has allowed me to be a part of your lives in some way. I encourage you to never give up on your dreams, to take goal setting through masterminding seriously, and to watch the fruits of your labor come to fruition. I am honored to have each of you in my life, as every one of you has helped shape me into the master builder who builds master minds. Thank you.

Ann

Introduction

In this book and the companion workbook, I attempted to define my many years of consulting, coaching and life experiences while working with business organizations, associations, and individuals of all ages and all levels of accomplishments. I am fortunate to have accumulated wisdom, knowledge and understanding of why it is important to have a dream, a definite purpose, and a desire, because without them, your realization would not manifest.

When most people talk about having a dream come true, they're usually talking about a dream in one particular area of their lives. But what if you were able to have a dream come true in every area of your life? That is the focus of this book, having a dream come true in ten essential areas, not just one. This book was written and predicated upon the success principles contained in the book, 'Think and Grow Rich' by Napoleon Hill. In my book, I explain how you can have a dream come true spiritually, financially, in your family, health, education, personal development, business, recreationally, civics, and creatively. While being transparent, I share my personal successes and failures in each category, ending with how I am living a dream come true in each area of my life while consulting and sharing how you can do the same. One's ability to be able to balance the various aspects of their life and be successful in each of those areas is what makes them well-rounded.

Achieving your dream of prosperity in each area of your life through goal setting cannot be achieved over night. It has taken me years of planting seeds, then waiting for the harvest in order to fully realize my dreams. There is a strategy for success, and if you follow the strategy, you too can achieve success. If you commit yourself to your goals, constantly work on your realistic, yet challenging actions plans, apply frequent monitoring, develop self-discipline and be patient, then you can be secure in the knowledge that the end result will be as you designed it. In the final analysis, whether you realize it or not, each of us design our own outcomes regardless of what that outcome may be, success or failure. Some strategically design their lives, but others do it unaware and get the results of what comes to them by default. There is nothing in this world that you cannot accomplish if you have a system or a method in place and follow it.

It is my prayer that this book will be a blessing to all who read it from beginning to end. May your life be changed for the better after reading it.

"When any object or purpose is clearly held in thought, its precipitation in tangible and visible form is merely a question of time. The vision always precedes, and itself determines the realization."

Lilian Whiting

Table of Contents

1

Spiritual

The purpose of life is a life of purpose.
~Robert Byrne

When I started this journey of personal development, I did not know the purpose and the power of a strong spiritual foundation. That was the vision, mission and the dream to hold everything together. As a young girl growing up, I worked with my dad picking vegetables in the fields of the South. At the time, I did not know what I wanted to do when I grew up, but I did know that I didn't want to pick vegetables. After picking the vegetables, we would then sell them from the back of my dad's truck. We would also sell sandwiches. My friends from school would sometimes see me selling vegetables and sandwiches from the truck and would laugh at me. My father also had a lawn business where he would cut yards, so there were times that I went with him to help with the yards. When I got older and was in high school, I went from the vegetable fields to becoming a maid and a dishwasher at Singer Island Hotel in Riviera Beach, Florida. I cleaned the hotel rooms during the day and washed dishes in the kitchen at night at the same hotel. I did this every summer.

My mother was a holiness minster, so we were in church all the time. For example, we were in church seven days a week and twice on Sundays, literally. My mother was also a maid, so I felt that being a maid was my destiny too. Cleaning hotel rooms allowed me to see how wealthy people lived. I began to dream about what it would be like to be able to live that kind of lifestyle. When I returned home from working, I would help my mother with the house or with preparing dinner. She had taught me how to cook at a young age, so I also knew how to prepare meals. As a family, we always sat at the dinner table together to eat. If someone was not home, we would wait until they got there before we ate. Working in those various capacities prepared me for business and entrepreneurship. Unbeknownst to me, I was learning the habit of hard work, commitment, dedication, and perseverance. My mother also taught me the right way to cook and clean from a domestic standpoint, so my parents unknowingly taught me how to be well-rounded. My family did not have a lot of money, but I was blessed with parents who instilled many prosperity examples of what God could do for me *if* I had the faith to believe. My faith started as a wish, which turned into a dream, which turned into a burning desire, which turned into reality, and then, I experienced a dream come true. One of the things that I am learning about achieving a better quality of life is that it is built on four key strengths:

1. An intimate knowledge of what you want
2. A realistic time frame for when you want it
3. A definite plan for how you will get it
4. The desire to do whatever is necessary to achieve a positive outcome

The essence of life is a spiritual experience. In building on the foundation of your life, you must start with your spirit first, which is the divinity with you, which is where wisdom, knowledge and understanding is found. When God created man, He breathed into his nostrils, the "Breath of life" and man became a living soul, so the breath that is in you, is God's breath. His Spirit is inside you and is the foundation upon which your life is built. Without regular time with your Creator, your spiritual power will diminish, which can create cracks in the foundation of your life.

Do you face problems today because you have become so self-sufficient that you seemed to have forgotten that there is a God? Oftentimes we get caught up in our daily routines that we forget that there is an Omnipresent Power that is so much bigger and powerful than we could ever imagine, and we end up missing the mark. If we just follow the principles found in the Word of God and maintain a relationship with the Word Himself, we will find that our lives will become supernaturally guided down a path that leads to peace, prosperity, success, and abundance. That is the blueprint for obtaining prosperity and success through God. Having a relationship with Him is the formula. His plans for you are greater than you could ever imagine. Believe it or not, God's vision for your life is far greater than the dream you have for your own life. In the book of Jeremiah 29:11, it says, *"For I know the plans that I have for you, plans to prosper you and not harm you. To give you a hope and a future."* As my life became challenged, I began to study the Word of God more diligently and it became a great source of comfort for me. If you believe that the Word of God can change you as well, and you have faith, then you know that God wants you to have all the desires of your heart and more.

The Gift of Life

Have you ever given a gift to someone who showed little to no appreciation for it? You may have saved years to be able to buy that specific gift for that special person. You may have waited for just the right time to give them the gift. However, when they receive it, they open it, look at it, put it down and simply walk away without any acknowledgement or verbal expression or gratitude for what you gave to them. How would you feel? Would your feelings be hurt? Would you be devastated? This is how God feels about us when we take His daily blessings for granted and never bother to stop and thank Him. We ignore Him and all that He does for us each day and overlook His gift of life to us. He has given us the gift of life abundantly and some of us only take want we want and walk away without a simple "Thank you."

At one point in my life, that ungrateful person was me in my attitude towards God. I had not come to an appreciation of the abundant life that He had given me. I did not regard the blessings that He had bestowed upon me. That blessing that I speak of is the breath of life, yes "breath". Try not breathing and you will see what I mean. I had not even stopped long enough to thank Him for what He had blessed me with up to that point, until my life changed.

The Secret

I began my journey to a life of abundance by first facing adversities that were designed to make me stronger. I finally began to listen to the still small Voice speaking to me through my spirit. I stopped and listened to the Voice. A major part of my journey began with a spiritual awakening and awareness that everything I desired would come to me through the Word of God. So, the journey began towards a pursuit of a life of living abundantly. I had always heard everyone talking about the "secret" to success. I was always searching for that secret. Then, I realized that there is no secret. I began to seek God's face regularly through prayer, meditation, and the study of God's Word. I began rising early just to spend time with Him and to ask for guidance concerning His plans for my life. I began asking Him to fill me with the knowledge of His will for my life. My life began changing as I put Him first. I soon found out that a relationship with God is the secret.

Learning Through Tests

There were stumbling blocks, obstacles, and disappointments along the way as I grew in my faith. Nevertheless, I continued to be steadfast and hold on to the faith I had as it grew stronger each day. My commitment to spiritual growth kept me focused. I learned that there is a cost to be paid before any reward is given. Little did I know however, that I would experience trials, tribulations, sufferings, a divorce, devastations, betrayals, illnesses, loss, hurts and disappointments that awaited me. However, they each birthed wisdom, knowledge, understanding and resilience in me and for me, characteristics that would be needed for future and greater experiences, both good and bad. The patience that was needed and eventually manifested in the face of obstacles and setbacks became my most valuable asset. While God is working things out in your life, it is important to be patient. The problem with most is that we want what we want and when we want it, but God is doing something in you as you wait, so although it may seem frustrating having to wait, that wait time is producing something far greater in you. It is not always what happens to you, but rather, what happens "in" you that really matters. God knew this, which is why He instructed in His Word to be anxious for nothing (Philippians 4:6-7). We must realize that through longsuffering, life's greatest rewards are reserved for those who do not weaken in the face of adversity and whose patience is not worn out by waiting. Patience indeed is a virtue.

Wisdom

Increase in me that wisdom, which discovers my truest interest; strengthen my resolution to perform that which wisdom dictates. (Ben Franklin.) Wisdom of the ages is found within the pages of the Bible. The "Word" is all you need to understand how to deal with life's issues, challenges, and situations. The real secret is that there really is no secret. All that needs to be done is to act upon what you read and apply what you learn. This is easier said than done. The *application* of what you read must be made. The principles found in the Bible have withstood every test of time throughout the ages. Every book that has or will ever be written on universal principles and laws is founded upon Biblical principles. Every other book simply replicates, duplicates, and reiterates what is already found within those sacred pages. Napoleon Hill proudly admitted that his success principles were taken from Biblical principles and that he simply applied those principles when building his success empire. I realized that wisdom acquired through the

Word is more valuable than any material possessions that I had desired.

In the book of James, Chapter 1:5-7, the following is written for those who do not have, but desire to have wisdom: *If any of you lack wisdom, let him ask of God, that gives to all men liberally, and upbraideth not; and it shall be given him. But let him ask in faith, nothing wavering. For he that wavers is like a wave of the sea driven with the wind and tossed.* Wisdom is a gift that God gives to those who ask for it. It is also given to those who seek the Lord's will in spirit and in truth. Those who ask for wisdom and who remain close to their Creator will receive this priceless virtue. Wisdom teaches you what to say and when to say it, how to act and how to react, when to enter and when to exit, when to speak and when to keep quiet. Everyone does not have wisdom. Some who may have common sense may think that they have wisdom, but there is a difference between common sense and wisdom.

Common sense is practical judgment concerning everyday matters or a basic ability to perceive, understand and judge in everyday matters. Common sense is birthed from experiences and observations of the world. Wisdom on the other hand, is deeper insight or understanding that transcends the ordinary, often associated with discernment of moral, ethical, or religious matters. It is a guidance that comes from God offering profound insights into life. Spiritual wisdom guides you towards inner peace and a closer relationship with God. Through wisdom, a house is built. As we continue to strive to accomplish goals, to find peace, to connect with God and increase our faith, wisdom is the essence that will lead to significant growth in all of those areas. It was through praying for and applying wisdom in my decision-making that I avoided many pitfalls. When I did make mistakes, it was through wisdom that I was able to overcome them and learn valuable lessons.

Prayer

As a Christian, the foundation of my spiritual life is predicated on prayer. The Bible clearly instructs us to pray. The

Word of God teaches that if our prayers are effectual and fervent, they will avail much. Many Christians were taught to pray as children, but as adults, do you still pray consistently? Do you really believe in the power of prayer? …and do you truly understand what prayer is? It is nothing more than communicating with your Creator. It is also the doorway into the spiritual world. It is how you access God. Prayer is centered around relationship. God wants to hear from His children. He wants you to go to Him with your concerns and supplications. When you pour out your heart to God in prayer, in the name of Christ, that pleases Him because He desires that His children have open communication with Him. Included in prayer can be praise, worship, and interceding for others. Prayer is not only asking God for things but approaching His throne with humbleness of heart and meekness of spirit. God hears and hearkens to the prayers of His children. From the secret place of prayer, comes powers that shake the world. How often do you pray?

Faith

Faith is the cornerstone of Christianity. The Bible teaches that we have been justified by faith, and because of this faith, we have peace with God through our Lord Jesus Christ. It is by faith that we have access into grace. Many Christians claim to have faith, but when it is time to use that faith in trying situations, many fall short. At some point in life, you will be tested in every area that you claim you believe. Faith that is untested and untried is not true faith and has little credibility. When the times of testing and trials come, and they will come, will your faith be strong? Will the words that come out of your mouth during the times of trials and trouble line up with your professions of faith, or will your own words testify against you? True faith leads to peace, which leads to victory. According to the Word, it is by faith that we understand that the worlds were framed by the Word of God. It was by faith that Abraham received a great inheritance. It was by faith that Mary received the words of the angel Gabriel that she would bring forth the Messiah, Jesus Christ. True faith goes into operation when there are no answers. To have faith means believing the unbelievable. How strong is your faith?

The First Mastermind Group

Andrew Carnegie, the billionaire industrialist was Napoleon Hill's mentor and deposited within him everything he knew and had learned about prosperity, success, financial wealth, and abundance. During an interview, Napoleon Hill once asked Andrew Carnegie the question, "What is a Mastermind Group". He asked this question since Mr. Carnegie had attributed most of his success to his affiliation with his Mastermind Group. Mr. Carnegie answered Napoleon Hill's question by giving an example of what he called the first Mastermind Group in the world, which was Jesus Christ and His disciples. He went on to explain how Jesus had met frequently with his disciples to discuss love, forgiveness, prayer, salvation, and the vision that was to be carried out for the salvation of the world. Jesus and the disciples were the first Mastermind Group. According to Andrew Carnegie's definition, a mastermind group is, "an alliance of two or more minds working together in perfect harmony towards the attainment of a definite objective." No successful person has attained great success by themselves. Every mind needs association and contact with other minds by which to grow; hence, a mastermind Group.

Pursuing worldly possessions such as money, power, fame, and fortune may provide temporary satisfaction, but ultimately, those things cannot compare to the value of your soul. Many people today are caught up into chasing after material things, often neglecting their spiritual well-being in the process. Some even resort to selling their souls in exchange for money and fame, only to find out that they have traded something of infinite worth for things that are ultimately meaningless. On Judgment Day, all of the material possessions that people have acquired will be of no use or value to them. Material things decay. Moth and rust will eventually destroy all material things. Possessions cannot be taken with you to the other side, and you cannot use them to buy your way out of judgement. In contrast, the state of your soul will determine your eternal destiny. As believers, it is crucial to keep your soul spiritually fed and nourished. The pursuit of money, power, fame, and fortune should not take precedence over the well-being of your soul. On Judgment Day, you will not be judged by how much you have accumulated in this world, but by the condition of your soul. Are you balanced in the area of Spirituality?

My Process for Spiritual Growth

Many years ago, I created a spiritual growth process that I called my daily date with myself. This includes rising early in the morning between 3:00-4:00a.m. to pray, meditate, read, journal, write my lessons learned from the previous day, write the desires of my heart for the current day, list two-three things that I am thankful for, two-three things that I am grateful for, and asking the Spirit to give me ten opportunities for the day. This information can be found in my book entitled, 'A Daily Date with Myself.'

Builders Toolbox 

- ❖ In what ways does your faith influence your actions and decisions, especially during trials and tribulations?

- ❖ Have you experienced a time when self-sufficiency caused you to overlook the presence and guidance of God?

- ❖ How can maintaining a relationship with the Word of God lead to a life of peace, prosperity, success, and abundance?

- ❖ How has facing adversities strengthened your spiritual journey and relationship with God?

- ❖ How consistent are you in your prayer life, and what impact has it had on your spiritual and personal growth?

You Must have a Dream!

What is your spiritual dream? Write it down.

2
Family

What is your dream in the area of your family? What would you like to see come true in this area? My method of goal setting and planning has its origins many years ago when I became success conscience. There is no secret to achieving success. But you must have a dream to have a dream come true. If there is no dream, then what is it that will manifest into your life? Since discovering that there is no secret, but learning that there is a system, and applying that system in my own life daily, I discovered that the system works if you work it. Once I realized that the system worked, I had a sense of urgency to share the system with as many people as possible, starting with my family.

Imagine that you are the pilot of an airplane. It's early in the morning and the sun is just rising. You are sitting in the cockpit of a 747 preparing to lift off. You check with your co-pilot (your significant other) to make sure that everything is in place and ready for takeoff. You check the controls, then you begin to taxi down the runway. The sky is clear, and it is one of the most beautiful days you have seen in a while. All the passengers are buckled in, and they are all depending on you to get them safely and timely to their destination. There is only one problem. You have no idea where you are taking them. Where are you going? What is the family flight plan? You are the pilot in your family, and everyone is looking to you to have the flight plan for their lives, your significant other and your children. They are all looking to you. The flight plan is your family's mission statement and the vision for where you want them to go, how they will get there and by when. They are all looking towards you for guidance spiritually, financially, personally, educationally, health wise, etc. Do you have the plan for everyone?

Family Vision/Mission Statements

Oftentimes, we as individuals have a clear vision and/or mission in mind for our own job or company, and actually go the next step by writing that vision and mission down in the form of an affirmation, but rarely do we write a vision or mission statement for our lives. In creating a viable vision/mission statement for your family, you must begin with the end in mind by having a clear vision of your family, how you see them in the future and how they will get to where they need to be. The question is, how do you apply the principle of bringing the vision to fruition? The creating of your family's mission statement is a good place to begin. In his book, Seven Habits of Highly Effective Families, Stephen Covey quotes that, *A family mission statement is a combined unified expression from all family members of what your family stands for, what it is that you really want to do and be as a family, and the principles you choose to govern your family life. It borders on the idea that all things are created twice. First comes the idea or the mental creation, then comes the reality or the physical creation. It is the blueprint before constructing the building.*

When you create a mission statement for your family, you are actually taking charge of the future for generations to come. You are deciding what kind of family you want to be and have, and you are also identifying and applying the principles that will help you become that family. Having a vision and mission for your family impacts the decisions that each family member will make. This will contribute towards making your dream come true in the area of your family. Remember that prosperity comes when the steps made to reach success are applied. Begin the process now to develop your family's mission statement. Start by creating a vision of what you want your family to be like and what principles you will stand on. This is a family affair. It does not matter if there are only two, three or more people in your family, everyone must participate, even if you have adult children. The 'McNeill Family's Mission Statement' is as follows:

As a family, we are loving, peaceful, patient and kind to each other. As a family of speakers, we speak to share with the world. Our generosity is shared with others as we live a life of significance while leaving a family legacy.

As you collaboratively develop a family mission statement and you begin masterminding with your family, remember to create spiritual goals. It is a wonderful thing to mastermind with your family and enjoy all of the benefits that come with it, but if not careful, as a family, you can become too engrossed in the family goals that you lose sight of the One who made it all possible, God. Therefore, it is vitally important that the family is spiritually balanced. This is done with the inclusion of the spiritual category when developing family goals.

Family Bonding

A quality family life requires quality family time. In today's modern world, the idea of family time has become a thing of the past. Very few families sit at the dinner table and eat together, have discussions about their day and just sit and talk with no cell phones in view. In this technologically advanced digital world that we live in, everyone for the most part, is always connected to their cell phones, social media, and other electronic devices. As a result, the family members have become distanced from each other. Don't let that happen to you and your family. Be deliberate in creating a family vision and mission statement and be deliberate in spending quality time together. One mistake I made was that I was committed to my personal goals, but I did not have goals for my family, and this caused problems in my marriage.

Family Affirmations

An affirmation is different from a vision and mission statement, in that it specifically affirms who we are (in the family), what we do and what we have as a family unit. These affirmations may not have come into reality just yet, but they are written in the present tense spoken as a "now" reality. Family affirmations are like daily deposits which help to strengthen the family unit, in particular the children, because we are constantly depositing images into their minds, and they come to believe that they actually are who they continuously hear themselves to be by others. This is why we must be strategic when speaking to and over our children. As a parent, would you withhold food from your child for days, weeks, or months? I certainly hope not. Well, consider how many days, weeks or months go by without us depositing positive affirmations to our children.

What about your spouse or other loved ones? Do you affirm them? Affirming and showing my husband that he is the most important person in my life has given me a marriage of contentment and peace. No, we are not perfect and neither is our marriage, but we are committed to our marriage and our family. It is not just about you being affirmed, but you affirming others as well. There may be someone who needs to hear how talented they are, how skillful they are, how much of a blessing they are to you. Those are deposits that you make into the lives of others. A family mission/vision statement and a family affirmation help to create balance in the family. Is your family balanced? If not, make plans to become balanced through the development of family vision/mission statements and affirmations. Masterminding with my family has given me the love, support, constant laughter, and open communication between us that I could not even ask for. I am living my dream come true in the area of my family.

A Family Affair

Before you start a mastermind group with others, consider starting one with your family first. If at all possible, take immediate steps to involve your family from the beginning. The learning experience will be deeper, the bonding will become stronger, and the insight and joy will become greater when you begin to discover and share things together. By masterminding with your family, you will not find yourself leaving your spouse or children behind, but everyone will be growing together. This way, they won't feel threatened by your desire to want to grow, change, and elevate yourself because they will be too focused on their own desires to be changed and elevated as well.

Napoleon Hill once said that one of the greatest mastermind groups is one with a husband and wife masterminding together for a definite chief purpose for the family. Learning together can be a powerful force in helping to build a stronger and better family unit. After 30 years of masterminding my own life and coaching others, I am learning that when people go through the masterminding process as a family, it makes a stronger family unit. The bond is strengthened through reading, having meaningful discussions, and sharing back and forth. As time goes on, the family gets new insights, new learning, and the understanding of each other grows. It starts a process that is truly exciting. The spirit is yoked together in the family. Your duty to your family is to do something every day to increase motivation to the members in your family. Consider your mate if you have one, and the mastermind relationship between the two of you. Try rekindling your enthusiasm as you did when you first met while remembering that tomorrow is not promised. You want to live a life without regrets.

Family Drama

I grew up in Riviera Beach, Florida at 1408 W. 36th Street. Later, my family moved to 1449 W. 28th Street in Riviera Beach. We moved because my father's sister convinced him to purchase a duplex with her. This would allow our two families to live side by side in a larger family residence, but all under one roof. My father initially was going to purchase a single family home but decided to purchase the duplex with his sister and his mother, who were my aunt and grandmother. My mom, dad and brother were on one side of the duplex and my aunt and grandmother were on the other side. It was wonderful. We all lived happily together. That was, until my father passed. Soon after his death, my aunt approached my mother and said to her, *"Now, you need to pay me rent."* Rent? ... on a house that we had already paid off over a period of thirty years? My aunt had never added my father's name to the deed. I was about 24 years old at the time, so to keep the peace, I paid rent to my aunt for my mother to continue living there, until my aunt passed away. After her death, the family drama got worse. My aunt had willed the property to two people: a relative and my firstborn, who at the time was five years old. Since the property was left in a will, we were in probate court for 15 years, only to finally lose the property in the end. The blessing in disguise from all that family drama was the wealth of knowledge that I acquired about probate, trusts and family. As a result of this knowledge, I have been able to help many people through probate situations, although I am still learning about these things.

In August of 2024, I tried to purchase that same family property to hold on to my childhood home, but the price was too high at $250,000. However, the owner gave me the backstory concerning that property and all the things that had happened so many years ago. I had no idea that there was so much that had taken place over one property. This all happened because there was no trust in place all those years ago. What I want you as a reader to take from my experience is to NOT find yourself in the same situation. The four points below will save your family so much money, drama, and headaches if taken care of now:

- Anything that requires a change of title, should never be put in a will. For example: a car, bank account, house, portfolio

- Anything that requires a change of title should be put in a trust

- If you plan on leaving anything that requires a change of title to only **one** person, then you must add their names to everything now (i.e: car, bank account, house, portfolio, etc.) prior to your passing (otherwise those things will go to probate court for a change of title).

- If you plan on leaving anything that requires a change of title to more than one person, then you must hire a trust attorney prior to your passing so that he or she can create a trust to place everything in.

This next situation happened to me three times, but I will share only one. My uncle, my mother's brother was hospitalized, and as his health began to deteriorate, so we went to visit him in St. Petersburg, Florida. While there, I asked the hard question about who would be taking care of his burial from a financial standpoint, only to find out that he was uninsured and that his children did not have the finances for his final arrangements. That responsibility fell on me, and I ended up having to take care of everything. The lesson learned from this experience was to ask questions sooner rather than later. If you think that you may be the person who will be financially responsible for a loved one when they pass away, then ask questions now to find out if they have things in place. If no-one else in the family is identified to take care of things, then work with them to make arrangements sooner rather than later. (There is more on this subject in my other book entitled, 'Remember me This Way')

Family Matters Most

On the stair step of life, you must remember your family. One day my brother drove me to a funeral in Tampa for a close friend whose mom had passed away. While on the drive, we talked of old times, current times, and the future. At that moment, I realized how I knew so much about so many others, but very little about my own family members. My brother has five children. There are four girls and one boy. His son has five children and only one daughter has one child. As I began to ask for an update on each child, I realized that they were all grown up. While on the stair step of life, we must get off every now and then and remember the many steps along the way, as they each represent years and lives lived and living, past, present and future. Family matters most at the end of the day. As my brother continued to drive, we both made a new commitment to each other to do a better job of keeping in touch, because family matters most, no matter what has happened in the past.

A Dream Come True

Over 20 years ago, I set a goal to partially retire by the time our youngest daughter was out of high school, then totally retire by the time she was out of college. The specific goal stated was, *"By December 31, 2008, my husband and I both will be retired and have no major debt."* On January 2, 2009, at 5:00a.m., my husband and I went for our daily walk in the park. While walking, he said to me, *"I'm not going back to work."* I thought he meant that he was not going back to work that day, but when we got back home, he wrote a letter to his employer of thirty years that said, *"Effectively immediately, I am retiring. Please pack up my things and have them mailed to my home."* The irony of the story is that I had not shared my goal or desire of retiring with him by December 31, 2008. Here it was the first week of 2009, and he retired on his own without me verbalizing my desire. It seemed as though he picked up my desire for us to retire together. Although it happened a week after my target date, it still happened. Better a week late than never. That was a dream come true for me and I didn't even see it coming.

Family Rituals

In the McNeill family, dinner time is our most sacred time together. As previously stated, in most modern families today, eating together at the dinner table has gotten lost. The children may eat in their rooms or in the living room in front of the television, dad may eat on the run, mom may be the only one who eats at the dinner table alone or in the kitchen leaning over the counter. However, eating together is extremely beneficial for bonding and strengthening the family unit. And this simple, yet powerful family practice has impactful and far-reaching benefits for each member in the family, even if only done once or twice a week. Another family ritual was Sunday worship. For years, when our children were younger, we would all worship together. This family ritual came from my own family because I was born in a holiness family, and we were in church all the time. Because of this, I could not wait to go to college, so I did not have to go to church every day; so while in college, I would sleep in and party with my friends, but the seed was planted and growing, and the pruning time would come later in life when the challenges of life and God brought me back to my knees to worship. Another family ritual was watching our family's favorite TV shows, such as 60 minutes and also attending movies and sports events togethers.

As my two daughters grew older and then my grandson came along, we continued this ritual with him. One of the activities we would do at the dinner table is to take turns sharing highlights of our day. Although we recognized that this ritual kept our family close, we had no idea of the tremendous impact that it had on our grandson Malachi, so much so, that while traveling to Uganda with him, we had dinner with a small group of friends. While at dinner, Malachi, who was ten years old at the time, boldly and confidently asked the dinner guests one by one, *"So what was the highlight of your day?"* Somewhat surprised, the first guest answered and told him what his was. Then he went around the table until he had reached the last person. Eventually, he shared the highlights of his own day. After he had finished, someone asked him what made him do that, and he said, *"This is what we do at home."* He thought that it was normal for everyone to do that at the dinner table, therefore, he didn't think it was odd when he initiated it with guests who were friends of mine. What are some family rituals that you hold dear?

A Family Belief System

Marva Collins in her book entitled Values says it well, *"Parents, teachers, and caregivers are the first molders of a child's belief system."* Everything we say and do is recorded on an invisible tape in a child's mind, which becomes part of their belief system. With this in mind, it is important to understand that children will do more of what they see us do than what they hear us say. Think of your actions, your words, and your beliefs as you contribute to their invisible recorders. How you handle problems in front of them, how you act when angry, how you and your spouse or partner interact with each other, how family members communicate, how you handle sadness or disappointment, everything contributes to molding them, and that recorder is always on. This recorder has no erasers. The power of your words and actions speak loudly in the lives of your family members inside and outside of your home.

The Importance of Balance

My husband is the most important person in my life and my desire is to express this through my daily actions. I try to constantly affirm him as well as practice it because there was a time that while climbing up the ladder of success, I found out that my ladder was leaning against the wrong wall. My career was first and everyone and everything else was second, and they felt it. My parents had instructed me to go to school, get a good education and then get a good corporate job. I did that, but then I realized early in my career that I needed to own my own business, but I also needed to strive for balance in every area of my life because my life was out of balance at that time. These areas needed to be in alignment, spiritual, family, financial, education, health, business and personal development because balancing these areas would maintain some semblance of balance in my life. As I grew in maturity and wisdom, I realized that prosperity and success do not amount to much of anything if the family is in shambles. Family is the foundation upon which the motivation to succeed should be built upon. A healthy family creates happy and confident members within the family. How about your family? What can you do to make your dream come true in the area of your family?

Successful families don't just happen. They take every bit of energy, talent, vision, determination, and rescue effort a person can muster. They take prioritizing, planning and sacrificing. They require family members to be willing to say, "I'm sorry" and to do whatever is needed to make adjustments. Yes, in times of storms or calm, families need someone who is prepared to step up and not give up. Someone who is ready to lead.
~Steven Covey

Builder's Toolbox 

- ❖ What is your dream for your family, and how do you envision it coming true?

- ❖ How do you involve each family member in setting and achieving family goals?

- ❖ What specific spiritual goals do you have for your family, and how do you plan to achieve them?

- ❖ Have you started a mastermind group with your family? If so, what benefits have you observed?

- ❖ How do you balance personal goals with family goals to avoid conflicts and ensure harmony?

- ❖ What family rituals do you cherish, and how do they contribute to family bonding?

You Must have a Dream!

What is your dream in the area of your family?
Write it down.

3

Finances

Real wealth is ideas plus energy.
~Richard Buckminster Fuller

The night my life changed was December 31, 1979 about 9:00p.m. This is when my dream began to unfold. I was 25 years old, married, and had one young child. Since it was New Year's Eve, my husband and some friends went out to bring in the New Year, but I decided to stay home and begin reading a new book that my physician had recommended to me. The book was called, Think and Grow Rich, by Napoleon Hill. As I began to read that book, that book began to read me! When I reached page 36, there were six statements requiring the reader to write down the answers to. I took out my pen and pad and eagerly attempted to answer each question. These questions started my life on a new trajectory. The statements were as follows:

Six ways to turn Desires into Gold:

The method by which desire for riches can be transmuted into its financial equivalent, consists of six definite, practical steps:

First: *Fix in your mind the exact amount of money you desire. It is not sufficient nearly to say, "I want plenty of money." Be definite as to the amount (there is a psychological reason for definiteness, which will be described in a subsequent chapter).* **My answer:** $1,000.00

Second: *Determine exactly what you intend to give in return for the money (there is no such reality as, "something for nothing.")* **My answer:** Save the money.
(At some point later on, I realized that my answer above was not the right answer).

Third: *Establish a definite date when you intend to possess the money you desire.* **My answer:** December 31, 1980 (One year from that date)

Fourth: *Create a definite plan for carrying out your desire, and begin at once, whether you are ready or not to put this plan into action.* **My answer:** I don't have a plan right now.

This is where it became challenging for me. In my mind, I thought that getting $1,000 would be relatively easy because all I needed to do was save $200 a month. It sounded simple enough. After all, my husband and I both had good salaries and we were not struggling financially, or so I thought. So, I began calculating my figures mentally at first, then I began writing them on a worksheet. Since I had a degree in accounting, I was pretty good at mental math; but when I analyzed my income v/s my bills, I realized that I was actually in the negative each month. There was no money left over! Why was I in the negative? I must have mentally calculated something wrong, but each time I redid it, the calculations were the same. I was in the negative each month.

Something wasn't right. Both my husband and I were college-educated adults working on advanced degrees, and we had good corporate jobs, owned a nice home, and seemingly had money for things we needed and wanted. But each time I worked out the numbers, I was still in the red! How was I going to save $1,000 if I was in the red each month? That's when I realized that my answer to question number two of saving the money was not going to be easy, based on what my financial situation was looking like. I had to first get out of debt when up until that point, I didn't even realize I was in debt. My mind went into overdrive. I came up with a plan, which was to secure a part time job at a fast food restaurant, but when I factored in the hours that I needed to work, considered the money that would be needed for childcare while at work, time to cook dinner, rest, spend time with hubby, and still work my regular full-time job, that plan was out of the window.

That night led me to me come up with so many other different plans and ideas to get those one thousand dollars, all of which were futile. After seeing no way to get this money, I began crying. As I sat there weeping, I asked myself why I was crying. It wasn't because I had no money, because for some reason, we were always able to buy what was needed and many of the things we wanted. I was crying because I saw no hope of getting out of financial debt. When I finally looked at the clock, it was 4:00a.m. Seven hours had passed! The New Year's Eve parties were over and, in walks my husband. He saw me sitting there with tears in my eyes and of course, he thought that I was crying over him coming in so late, so I let him think just that. The next two set of instructions from that chapter are listed below, but since I could not even get past question number two, I never made it to answering the last two questions.

> *Fifth: Write out a clear, concise statement of the amount of money you intend to acquire. Name the time limit for its acquisition. State what you intend to give in return for the money and describe clearly the plan through which you intend to accumulate it.* (I was not able to do this.)

> *Six: Read your written statement aloud, twice daily, once just before retiring at night, and once after arising in the morning. As you read, see and feel and believe yourself already in possession of the money.* (I was not able to do this just yet.)

That night changed my life. It was my first young adult wake-up call to the reality that while I had been climbing the ladder of what I thought was "success", the ladder was actually leaning against the wrong wall for me. I thought I had been doing all the right things. When we were children, our parents told us to finish high school, get a good education, go to college, earn a degree, then get a good corporate job in order to be (what is perceived as) successful. I did that. My husband did that. So why was I sitting there with more bills left over at the end of each month than money?

So, what do I do now was the question? My answer for that moment was to continue reading the book that I had soaked with tears. Although I was discouraged from my inability to appropriately answer the questions, I still continued to read. I read, read, and read some more. Although I had come to a stumbling block, I did not allow that to detour me from the motivation of pursuing a higher level of prosperity, success, and abundance that the book was teaching. After finishing Think and Grow Rich, I became extremely inspired, in spite of that financial reality check that I had received. Although my financial situation had not changed, somehow, I knew that my life had, and so the journey began. The book awakened a part of my inner being that propelled me to embark upon meaningful goals. I began planting seeds that manifested years and even decades later in my life. My dream was birthed after completing the book and it became clearer as each day, week, month, and year passed.

Renewed Motivation

Was my dream possible within the pages of what I had read? What must I do to be able to save one thousand dollars in a year? I never let my vision of acquiring this money die. I held it close and became very acquainted with the 13 principles of success described in Think and Grow Rich and I worked hard at implementing those principles into my life. I questioned if success was really a science of carefully organized facts and details, as Napoleon Hill had taught in the book. My new journey took me many places spiritually, mentally, and physically. For days, weeks, months and even years later, I continued the path of reading other motivational books that emphasized the principles and philosophies of Napoleon Hill in, Think and Grow Rich, and I continued to focus on saving my $1,000.00, which was my ultimate goal, desire and dream. It literally took me ten years to save that money because I had to get out of debt! That goes to show just how deep in debt I was. Could the application of the science eventually lead me to my dream of saving a thousand dollars? Could I really obtain my goal?

After having read Think and Grow Rich that night in 1979, it changed my life and my outlook on life. I continued to give away books to my friends who mostly attended the same church as I did. One by one, they began to yield to my request to develop a "definiteness of purpose" and discuss what kind of an impact (if any) the book had on them. My motivation continued to grow for years after reading that book, and I continued giving copies of the book to people as gifts. Not realizing it, I sometimes gave a copy to the same person. That did not matter to me. I just wanted people to feel the inspiration and motivation that I had been experiencing. I knew that something was happening in my life. Although conditions *seemed* to be the same, something was brewing in the spirit realm concerning me. I could feel it! I refused to let the inspiration go. I was so eager to prosper and grow that I found myself embracing a change in mindset as I continued to be drawn to the power of holding on to a definite purpose.

Young Matron's Mastermind Group

After church, me and some of the young women would get together to socialize. At our social get-togethers, we ate and talked about our children, families, the church, jobs, school or whatever was on our minds or happening in our lives at the time. This is where I would talk about and give away the book Think and Grow Rich. Some of the ladies in our social group were in their early to late 20s. Some were recently married with children, and some were single. Everyone had a desire for something different, a better quality of life. Many of us had dreams deferred, like a raison in the sun. I personally wanted a better relationship with God and my husband, I mean my husband and my God. I learned that as young women, we sometimes mistake our husbands for our Gods. There was no definite goal or purpose for the gatherings at first other than to socialize and have a place to let our hair down. I eventually realized that our get-togethers needed a focus and needed to be mind-stimulating because we were only socializing and catching up, and not doing much else. With this in mind, we formalized the group and called it, The Young Matron's Group. Without realizing it, I was unknowingly developing my first Mastermind Group. This was in 1980. Although we were relatively young, we became very focused.

As we grew spiritually, mentally, and personally, we began to set our dreams higher. One by one, the women developed their definite purpose and seriously began to consider how they would go about achieving their goals. We began discussing the principles contained in, Think and Grow Rich and talk about how we were going to apply them to our individual lives. We became very serious about taking our lives to the next level. Very rarely did we encounter challenges or personality conflicts with each other. For the most part, there was a spirit of harmony that allowed each of us to soar. As years passed, we grew in different directions, and we also grew collectively as a group. We began to lightly hold each other accountable and supported each other in our seen and unseen potential. We developed the ability to recognize the greatness and power of each mind.

We wrote our individual personal affirmations consisting of the person that we individually aspired to become. I went deep inside myself and identified the ideal "me." I wrote down what that person looked like, how she behaved, how she talked, how she made her money, what kind of businesses she operated, how she raised her children, how she bonded with her family, how she treated her husband, her friends, and most importantly, how she maintained her relationship with God. I memorized my affirmation and repeated it twice a day and so did every member in the Young Matrons Mastermind Group. I loved surrounding myself with those ladies and enjoyed the fellowshipping experience we shared. I began to see the power that the application of the principles from Think and Grow Rich had in my life. Since I was the poster child and greatest advocate for that book at that time, the women were looking for the manifestation of the principles in my life first, so I held myself accountable. I had a strong motive for wanting to follow the principles outlined in the book and I wanted my Mastermind Group to have that same enthusiasm. The power of this enthusiasm drove me to be, and later have peace that surpasses all understanding.

In time, many of the 10-12 women in the group began to experience great successes in their lives personally, family wise, and also in their businesses and careers. Some went on to become entrepreneurs, lawyers, real-estate agents, governmental supervisors and one even became a judge. When I look back, I realize that the meetings with those young women laid the foundation for what is now, *The International Mastermind Association*, located in Miami, Florida, where I currently am the president/founder. This organization has now grown into the international global voice of Masterminders. God used our individual life experiences back then as the foundation for a new way of living, a life of rich abundance by being accountable to each other.

As I began to focus on my spiritual and financial growth, my life began to take on a new meaning. My spirituality became a priority in life and my relationship with God became paramount. I continuously thought about my *"Definiteness of Purpose"* everyday, which is the first principle in Think and Grow Rich. I continued to conceive different plans and actions toward achieving my personal goal of saving $1,000 a year. The outward realization of my financial situation was that I could not save the first $1,000.00 until I got my debt under control by paying down some bills and creating new income streams as an entrepreneur. The goal of saving the one thousand dollars and the seeming inability to be able to realistically do it, led me to the realization of the fact that I needed to learn how to make money and have that money work for me. I finally began to understand what the scripture in James 2:14 meant when it says, "Faith without works is dead." I took it a step further and said to myself that, "Work without faith is dead too." This became my personal motto. So, I was ready to work with faith. I had the unwavering commitment that I would be able to save the money. I just needed a workable action plan. It has been said that any dominating desire, plan, or purpose backed by the state of mind known as faith is taken over by the subconscious mind and acted upon immediately, so I acted. I could see the money before my eyes. I could touch it with my hands. I believed in my heart that it was awaiting transfer to me in the spirit in which I delivered the service. I was simply waiting for the manifestation out of the mental world into the natural world. That conviction began to sink into my subconscious mind.

In the area of finance, we must have a dream to have a dream come true. But we must also study to show ourselves approved. The challenge I found in the area of my finances, was a lack of knowledge regarding money, how it multiplies, how it compounds, how to invest it, how to save it, how to spend it, what to spend it on, etc. Even though I had degrees in accounting and finance, I had never been taught about personal finances and investing. While in college, I learned about financial statements, accounting principles, cost analysis, taxations, auditing, micro and macroeconomics, but they did not teach me about personal financing and investing. My ignorance in personal finance was part of the reason that I was deeply in debt before learning about investing and how to handle money. We perish and suffer for lack of knowledge in every area of our lives.

After my first read of Think & Grow Rich, the realization that my mind must become "money conscious" in order to grow financially, while removing all fear and doubt about poverty became crystal clear. When you demand riches for yourself, you must be extremely clear about what riches you expect. To achieve your financial dreams, you must know what you want from a financial standpoint. In other words, what's most important about money to you and your family? Exactly how would you use the money? Financially, you must study to show yourself approved.

Financial Self-discipline

After realizing that there was more to finances than what I had learned in college, I began my quest towards educating myself about money, how to make money, how to invest it, how to sustain it and how to compound it. Henry Ford once said, *"Anyone who stops learning is old whether they are 20 or 80"*, so I continued to learn, especially about investing. Anyone who keeps learning, stays young. Regardless of how old we get, we must always keep the mind young. Once you make the decision to do this, the way will present itself.

I had decided to save $1,000 a year and that new goal started my journey towards reading and learning how to save and invest. The dream alone for financial success and security is not enough. It must be connected to self-discipline, personal values, and action. Therefore, the first step for me was to identify my debt. The next step was to be honest about how much I could pay each month towards that my $1,000 a year goal. After that, I committed to developing self-discipline to set aside a small amount to save, which started with $20 a month. Later I learned through reading investment books and joining an investment club to invest an additional $20 a month. Being self-disciplined compelled me to study and save when I did not feel like doing it. The Greek philosopher Plato stated, *"The first and best victory is to conquer self,"* and although this requires moral strength and mental fortitude, it can be done. Glenn Bland, the author of Success: the Glenn Bland Method, also helped to launch my personal journey on how to set goals and create action plans involving saving and investing. The application of goals setting and planning are the magic keys to happiness and success. Statistics show that only 3% of people have written specific, identified goals and plans. Ten percent have goals and plans but keep them in their head. The 87% drift through life without any goals or plans. They do not know where they are going, and others dictate to them; so the Glenn Bland plan that I followed was a simple way to learn how to accumulate money through applying his seven steps.

1. Do not charge
2. Do not consolidate your bills
3. Do not buy impulsively
4. Establish a budget
5. Pay yourself first
6. Pay monthly bills this way:
    - church or worthy charity
    - savings
    - insurance for security
    - food
    - shelter
    - all other things

In following those steps, I found that true happiness was not found in the possession of things. It could only be achieved by living a better quality of life with values and a plan of action. Saving and investing became a habit when I fixed in my subconscious mind a desire for financial freedom.

It's Never Enough

A man's life does not consist only in the abundance of things or the possessions he acquires. In the desire for money, one must also have spiritual discernment and an understanding of the values that drive your heart's desires. You must also identify your motivation about the decisions for money and what's important about money to you. Many small business owners are obsessed with money and think that it is the answer to every problem. At one point in my life, I thought that way as well and as such, I was driven by money alone. It became my obsession and the pursuit of it caused me to have tunnel vision, neglecting other things in my life that truly mattered, such as my marriage and my health. Many people have lost their families and friends and have ended up broken and miserable because of the pursuit of money. They acquired the money but lost things far more valuable that money cannot buy. This is why balance is essential. Pursue the money, but simultaneously pursue personal things that matter, such as your marriage, your children and quality time. Bill Bachrach, author of Values-Based Financial Planning, shares a five-step approach to help making it easier for business owners to have a better understanding of why money is important. Below are the five steps that Bill Bachrach identifies for business owners to understand why money is important.

1) Identify your values
2) Set your goals
3) Benchmark your financial reality
4) Create a financial blueprint
5) Educate yourself or seek an advisor

Values are important. There is a parable in the Bible that speaks of a rich fool. This story should be a lesson for us all. The story illustrated the error of believing that wealth can secure a person in all things, even the afterlife. In the parable of the rich fool in Luke 12, the man was materially blessed. His land "produced plentifully" and as God continued to bless him, instead of using his increase to further the will and kingdom of God, he was only interested in more increase and accumulating more wealth. He built larger barns in place of the existing ones and started planning an early retirement. Unbeknownst to him, that day was his last night on earth. Jesus then closed the story by saying, *"so is the one who lays up treasures for himself and is not rich toward God."*

The point of this parable is to understand that we are not to devote our lives to the gathering and accumulation of wealth, but to ensure that God is always at the forefront of all we do and to make sure that there is a balance between making money, serving God, and strengthening family bonds. Accumulating wealth should never be the number one focus. When we are obsessed with acquiring more and more and more, we are operating in greed. It does not matter what the "more" is. It could be money, clothes, material things, etc. Jesus encourages us all to explore some searching questions about ourselves. For example, we typically view certain sins as horrible because of their nature, but rarely do we view greed or covetousness as just as bad. Consider the term "greed" to simply mean a consuming desire for more and more and more, almost in a lustful, obsessive kind of way. With greed, no matter how much you acquire, it's never enough. Someone once asked John D. Rockefeller, *"How much money is enough?"* His reply was, *"one dollar more."* ...something to think about.

Birthing a Baby Billionaire

While in the second grade, our youngest daughter Ionnie started saving money in her piggy bank. I could see the proud look on her face when she would confidently place money in her piggy. Every month we would take her to the bank to make her deposits. By doing this, the seed for future investing was planted. She also learned about finances at a young age by listening in during the mastermind meetings each week. She was present during every meeting and took in all that she was hearing and learning, unbeknownst to me.

One particular Saturday morning as the last person in the mastermind group was finishing up their report and we were about to adjourn, eight year-old Ionnie said, *"Mommy, I want to give my report."* As her mother, I didn't even know she had a report, and this was the first time she had made this request. As we all looked at each other in pleasant shock, Mia, (one of the masterminders) said, *"Go ahead and share your report sweetheart."* Ionnie began to read: *Spiritually, I want to pray every day and read my Bible. Family: I want to be a good girl for my family. Education: I want to get straight As in school. Financially: I want to make lots of money. Recreation: I want to learn to play golf and basketball.* When she finished reading, we all were extremely shocked, impressed, yet proud of her. Everyone gave her a big hug. We can never estimate the degree to which children are being impacted by what they are exposed to, good, bad or indifferent. All those years of having her with me at mastermind meetings, conferences, other types of meetings and having her hear me talk about finances, investing and goal setting, all shaped and molded how she viewed and approached life, even until this day. As of this writing (January, 2025), Ionnie is now 34 years old.

Investment knowledge has power for every family, especially when it comes to generational wealth. This is something that we need to share with everyone. On the first day of the official formation of our Investment Club at Don Shula's Restaurant in Miami, Ionnie at nine years old was also joining an investment club with a group of children at the same location for their very first investment club meeting. After returning home, she asked me for the business section of the Miami Herald newspaper. As I handed it to her, she opened it to the stock section and found the page where Nike stock was listed. She sighed and said, *"Oh the price of Nike stock when down!"* Then she looked up at me and said, *"Now I know the difference between investing in Nike stock v/s investing in a pair of Nike shoes."* That was the beginning of our family's investment education journey and the birthing of the baby billionaire. As I stood in that kitchen approaching 50 years of age at the time, with two college degrees, the owner of two small businesses, I had not yet learned how to read the stock page with as much knowledge and understanding as this nine-year old had just done. The adult club focused developing bylaws while the children focused on learning about and how to read stocks.

At age 12, Ionnie began to annually max out her retirement account every year and continues to do so each year to this day. At age 17, she won the national competition award for Girls Going

Places, sponsored by Guardian Insurance. She beat out 5,000 girls who had also submitted their business ideas. Concurrently, she had begun to teach investing and how to analyze stocks as a volunteer of the National Association of Investors Club better known as Better Investing (for more information, and a 90-day free membership, go www.betterinvesting.org). She later began to brand herself as the Baby Billionaire and was featured on PBS and in magazines such as, Ebony, Black Enterprise, 17 Magazine, The Miami Herald, and many other media outlets. This was also the beginning of a new family culture of becoming more frugal and focusing on finances and financial empowerment (not financial literacy) as a family, all in the spirit of service to others.

As I continued to grow, I began to realize how to use the power within me to create opportunities that I needed in order to learn how to make money as an entrepreneur, rather than waiting every two weeks for a paycheck. My definite purpose of saving one thousand dollars began to cultivate character in me. An atmosphere in my life of determination for what I wanted emerged. I then began to draw willing supporters to me by having a positive mind and ridding myself of the spirit of procrastination, which had become a dominating bad habit it my life. I stopped measuring my future by my past and began to look forward to the positive that was in store for me. Negative thinking is what had me in a "poor" mindset which represented my past. I was not a bad person, just one who did not know how to elevate my thinking.

The House of Faith

From a financial perspective, your mind has no limitations, except for the limitations you create. You must have a dream to have a dream come true. Reading the book Think and Grow Rich elevated my level of thinking, cultivated optimism in me, and reading other books that stimulated my mind taught me how to dream and how to remove the limitations which were self-imposed in my mind regarding how much money I could actually earn; so how do you truly trust God for your dreams to come true? Is it by learning to build the dream, then trusting Him for it while working for it? I had dreamed of living in a beautiful home with sliding glass doors overlooking a pool and a golf course. This was the picture I had cut out and placed on my refrigerator years prior to my vision manifesting. I had learned to program my subconscious mind to attract to me whatever it was that I wanted.

One day, I decided to put my faith to work. I had been taking a course on how to buy a home with no money down and I decided to act on that idea. I called a friend to take me house shopping in a neighborhood that was very exclusive. In fact, it was the same neighborhood where Don Shula, the former Miami Dolphins Head Coach lived at the time. As I looked at the beautiful homes, my goal was to seriously consider only homes that were for sale by owners because I had bad credit, and I knew that owners would work with me more than real-estate agents would. During this time of my life, I had learned a valuable biblical principle, seek, *knock, and ask.* While reading in the book of Mathew, I realized that if I applied the *seek, knock, and ask* principle to the house, the car, the job, the project, the dream, and everything that I wanted, it may just work, so I applied the principle to buying a house in an exclusive neighborhood. …and I got the house, on the golf course! with no money down!

Our new home was 7,000 square feet, sitting on two golf courses with sliding glass doors overlooking an Olympic sized pool, a huge basketball court, a 1,000 square feet, gigantic upstairs balcony, off a master suite, a swing set in the back yard, six bedrooms, four bathrooms, three living rooms, two dining rooms, and a deck that extended the width of the home. Every morning, I would sit on the patio, which stretched the length of the house with my books, my hot cup of tea and a large chair to pray, read, meditate in nothing but silence. Beside me was my six-year-old daughter Ionnie, doing the exact same thing in her little lounge chair with her books and her hot cup of tea. This was the result of learning how to dream big and then magnetizing that dream to me. From Think and Grow rich, below are some steps to accumulating money:

1) Determine how much you desire.
2) Determine what you are willing to give in the form of a product or service in return for the money you desire.
3) Determine the exact date you want to have the money by.
4) Write a detailed plan of action.
5) Pay your tithes to God first.
6) Pay yourself second.
7) Create an automatic payment plan.
8) Invest automatically.
9) Pay your bills automatically.
10) Review your financial situation monthly.

Builder's Toolbox 

* What steps do I need to take to develop a clear plan for reaching my financial objectives?

* What are my spending habits, and how can I adjust them to better align with my financial goals?

* How can I increase my financial empowerment to make more informed decisions about money?

* How can I balance the pursuit of financial success with maintaining personal and family relationships?

* How can I ensure that my financial plans and goals contribute to a better quality of life and not just material wealth?

* What investments have I made that will have a financial benefit to my legacy in 20, 30, 40, 50 years from now?

You Must have a Dream!

What is your dream in the area of your
finances? Write it down.

4

Education

You and I will be the same in five years as we are today
except for two things, the books we read and
the people we meet.
~Charlie Tremendous Jones

What is the dream that you have for yourself in the area of continuous learning? Education is the lifelong process of acquiring knowledge, skills, values, and experiences that empower people to grow, adapt, and apply what they learn. Education goes beyond attending formal institutions and has to do with self-directed learning, practical life lessons, and the cultivation of critical thinking. Continuous learning should be a must in your life because it enables you to adapt, thrive, and stay relevant. In an era of rapid technological advancements and evolving industries, the knowledge and skills learned today may become outdated tomorrow. Continuous learning not only keeps you professionally competitive, but also enhances personal growth. In the journey of life, educational balance is required in order to keep your mind stimulated and to keep you on a path that leads to continuous learning. As long as you are still breathing, walking, talking and living, you are never too old to learn. However, when learning new things, you must ensure that the knowledge that you are embarking upon has a purpose for your life.

Show Yourself Approved

In the Bible, it says to, Study to show yourselves approved (Timothy 2:15). This passage applies to studying the Word of God, so that we will know for ourselves what God's plan is for our lives. However, this passage also applies to you studying other areas of your life that will enhance you and add quality to who you are as a person. You must always be studying something. What that is, is up to you, but reading and studying is essential. You must also have a reason for "why" you are studying and know what you will do with the newfound knowledge. How will your new knowledge enhance you as a person? How will this new knowledge assist you in teaching others? What is your purpose for seeking to learn new information?

Do you have a passion for doing something? Do you have a gift that not many others have? Consider your profession. Do you like it? Are you good at it? Do you want to get better at it? Study it! Study aspects of it that others in the field do not even consider studying. Are you willing to put in the time that others are not willing to put in, in order to become the best at what you love? Study it! Are you as knowledgeable in the industry as you should be or would like to be? Are you known in your industry locally or nationally for your knowledge? Are you the "go-to" person in your field? If not, ask yourself why or why not? Show yourself approved to those in your field, to yourself, and to others.

Specialized Knowledge

According to Napolean Hill, there are two types of knowledge: one is general and the other is specialized. After receiving my undergraduate degree in accounting from Florida Memorial University in May of 1976, I went to work at the Urban League of Miami. It was at that time that I had my sights on getting my master's degree and then my Ph.D because that was the path that everyone was taking. It was years later after reading Think and Grow rich, that I realized that I needed to specialize my knowledge because specializing in a certain subject was the way to make money. Education is the key to opening doors, but applying wisdom, knowledge and understanding can be the difference in what you do with your education once you enter those doors. For many years, I was taught to stay in school and get a good education so that I could get a good job and become successful, so I did that, but even after doing that, I was still deeply in debt. Years after reading many self-improvement books, I began to understand the meaning of specialized knowledge and the fact that my education needed to be specifically tied to my desire. I needed a niche in order to be rich in my area of expertise, which was the construction industry. I was working on another college degree, a master's in finance at Barry University in Miami twice a week at the time of reading Think & Grow Rich because that's what I was told that I should do. I was told that the more education one has, the more success they are likely to achieve. I was simultaneously in school at North Technical Trade School in Riviera Beach at night to learn about construction all while working my full time job at Pratt and Whitney Aircraft.

I understood that my degree would only allow me to make so much money in the corporate world, but with a trade, there was no limit to the amount that could be made as an entrepreneur. I went to college at night, and I attended trade school on the weekends. At the university, I was learning general knowledge related to finance, but at trade school, I was learning specialized knowledge in construction. I had both short term and long-term goals for my life. As I began to focus on my specialized area, my knowledge, competence, confidence, and self-worth began to increase. The power of specialized knowledge was a major "aha" moment for me while attending North Technical Trade School, because I began to learn how to build a house from the ground up. I also began to understand the power of competence while building confidence in that area of study. My confidence was one of many steps on that new journey of self-discovery as I explored a new field of study. That specialized knowledge eventually led me to taking the Florida State General Contractor's Exam. Resulting from my new knowledge, I started MCO Construction Company.

My desire for additional education in my vocation, my industry, my business, and my craft became more profitable as I applied my knowledge. Education for education's sake is meaningless; but to gain education in the area of a specialized field can become powerful and profitable, if properly applied with a specific goal in mind. I am continuing to learn that education is found not only in books, but also in continuing to acquire knowledge while organizing that information into a definite plan of action. The knowledge must then be directed into a plan of action to a specific end while developing and applying faith all along the way.

Get Your Education

Growing up Black, poor and in the segregated South, as a deprived youth in Riviera Beach, Florida, I thought the purpose of my early education was to be successful. I thought that educated, successful people seemed to be the ones who had the most money, such as movie stars, politicians, and business owners. They all drove luxurious cars and lived in big houses. I thought the more education one received and the more degrees they had, the richer they were. I can tell you now, that after having done all of that, and growing my construction business to focus on billion-dollar programs and going from being economically deprived to building a multi-million-dollar business, that success had little to do with my formalized education. The best education is found in studying and learning, then applying what you have learned. That is the true meaning of success. The most successful people in the world are not the richest or the most powerful. True education in life is learning that the successes in life are the people who enjoy living. They are the ones who find happiness everywhere. They look forward to every single day with excitement, enthusiasm, and joy. They love and they are loved. These are the most educated, most successful people. For example, mothers who may only have a high school diploma, who choose to stay home and raise her children, may be very successful also.

The Books you Read

My husband and I love to read. As our children and grandchildren grew older, from three years old, we would read to them, with them and encourage them to read to us. So now our youngest daughter has become a librarian out of her love for reading, now she gets paid to read. This is living. If we really understood the value that books bring to them, they would always keep a book with them. Continuous reading offers numerous benefits to the mind. First, it expands knowledge, exposes you to new ideas, cultures, and perspectives. This intellectual stimulation through reading enhances cognitive abilities, including critical thinking and problem-solving. Reading also nurtures creativity by introducing diverse narratives and concepts. It enhances vocabulary and language skills and improves communication by allowing you to contribute to a subject that you otherwise would not have any knowledge of had you not read on it. Reading books keeps the mind engaged and prevents cognitive decline as you age. Continuous reading is a powerful tool for mental development, cognitive growth, and overall well-being. It is important to note however, that in today's modern world, many no longer learn by reading hardcopy books. The way in which knowledge is acquired has evolved to audio books, podcasts, Tedtalks, videos, webinars, etc.

The invention of computers, Smart phones and other portable media devices have made it convenient to be able to listen to information while driving, waiting for a flight at the airport, waiting to be called at the doctor's office, etc. Podcasts have also gained popularity for their accessibility and the diverse content they offer. They are not necessarily books, but they offer a wide range of information to enhance knowledge. There is a litany of ways to acquire information. Just find a way to get new knowledge.

Diversify your Subject Knowledge

In finance, it is important to diversify your holdings in the creation of a balanced portfolio, depending upon your risk tolerance.

In life, it is important to diversify what you read. When I was a child, I read as a child, but as I became an adult, I began reading adult things. I realized the truism of Charlie Tremendous Jones who said: "In 5 years, I will be the same person except for two things: the books I read and the people I meet." Therefore, my experience has taught and continues to teach me that I must diversify my readings in various categories of my life. For example, prior to 1979 before I read Think and Grow Rich, I would only read books written by my favorite authors. I would check out books from the library regularly and read everything written by those particular authors, such as Maya Angelo, Norman Vincent Peale, and Og Mandino. After 1979, while on my journey of personal growth and development, the benefits of reading in different areas became clear to me. I began reading anywhere from 20-30 books a year.

Slowly, my reading began to shift my thinking as I began to cultivate a positive mental attitude. I began including spiritual books to my readings, which led me closer to God. Slowly, my financial focus became a priority as I read books on finance. How could I be so knowledgeable and diversified in so many areas through reading, yet still be deeply in debt? Those two elements do not harmonize. When one has knowledge, one must apply that knowledge to the areas with which they have acquired that knowledge. I began to apply the information that I was learning from reading books on finance. I began saving and investing and slowly pulled myself out of over a million dollars of debt. As I continued reading something every day, my readings became focused, strategic, and specific. After reading the book entitled, Success, by Glenn Bland, I reviewed the list of books that he had suggested at the back of the book, and my goal was to read each one that he had recommended, and I did, some were read twice. The list included, but is not limited to the following books:

- As a Man Thinketh (James Allen)
- The Magic of Thinking Big (David Schwartz)

- The Magic of Believing (Claude Bristol)
- The Greatest Salesmen Part 1 and part 2 (Og Mandino)
- How to Win Friends and influence people (Dale Carnegie)
- Acres of Diamond (Russel Conwell)
- The Millionaire Next Door

As I read each book in his list, I was enlightened by all of them. It was the same author Glenn Bland who educated me on how to prioritize other areas of my life by teaching me how to set goals and attach action plans to them in the areas of spirituality, family, financial, recreation and health. Later on, I expanded those areas of my life to include business, civic, creativity, educational, and personal development. I began setting goals in each of those areas and attaching my action plans to each goal that I set. The more you grow in different areas of your life, the more balanced you feel and the more success you will achieve towards the goals you set for yourself.

The Many Forms of Education

To echo Lincoln's words:
*"All that I am, and all that I hope to be,
I owe to my mother."*

My mama: I can still hear her voice clearly, quoting scripture and requiring me to learn to do the same. My mother never finished high school because she had to work as a laborer in the vegetable fields in Cordele, Georgia, but her education, wisdom, knowledge, and understanding came from the Word of God. Success principles and teachings from the Bible were instilled in me very early. As a child growing up, we were required to learn Bible lessons every Sunday. We were also required to learn scriptures, Bible verses and the 10 commandments. In order to master those lessons, scriptures, and commandments, we had to constantly practice them until we knew them inside out. This was the way my mother raised my brother, Karl Cobb and me. We were also required to learn how to read church announcements in front of the congregation, and we had to participate in church activities, which taught us leadership skills. Although my mother was not educated in the academic sense of the word, she was educated enough to teach me Biblical principles that were, and still are, embedded in me. Her education was that of spiritual wisdom, knowledge, Biblical standards and fearing the Lord. However, she did stress the importance of me getting my education.

It is evident that Past Secretary of state, Dr. Condolezza Rice understood the power of education very early in life when she shared her story at High Point University commencement in May, 2016 as their commencement speaker. She stated, *"In my family, starting all the way back to my grandparents, education was core to everything. My parents really believed that if you had a high quality education, there is nothing that you couldn't do. You are armored against segregation, armored against hatred, armored against prejudices, so the idea that you couldn't control your circumstances, but you could control your response to your circumstances, and education gave you a way to control that response. It was core to who we were."*

Education Through Failures

Education can also grow out of mistakes and weaknesses. My most memorable educational experiences did not come when things were well, but when things went wrong, when I made mistakes, and when I was challenged. For example, one of the lowest moments in my career was my lack of financial wisdom, which was my major weakness at the time. I was forced to learn how to save, invest, and study how to analyze stocks, not by choice, but by force because one day, I was introduced to a financial planner who knew that I did not know anything about investing. Therefore, I turned over to him my entire life savings of $15,000, which I had saved after many, many years; only to learn later that I would never see that money again. At first, I was upset with him, but the reality is that it was me who lacked financial education, even though I owned a business and had two business degrees. At that point, I chose to learn everything I could about becoming a smart investor. That $15,000 was the best financial education I could have ever received because it forced me to learn, to study, to show myself approved, and read books on finances. My educational weakness grew into an educational strength. As a result, we formed our first stock investment club and became members of The National Association of Investor's Corporation.

As my mastermind group continued to read and reread Think & Grow Rich, we added additional books on finances, such as, The Millionaire Next Door, The Automatic Millionaire, Die Broke and The Beardstown Ladies. Those financial books took our Mastermind Group into a direction that inspired the desire for more investment education and application of the financial education that we were receiving. This led to the development of an investment club called, Sisters Together Achieving Financial Freedom (STAFF). The STAFF Investment Club started with 22 Mastermind women. The club included ladies from diverse backgrounds and careers. Our goal was to learn how to save and invest by using an investment philosophy adopted from the National Association of Investors Club (NAIC). We formed our investment club, were educated by NAIC volunteers and learned how to analyze stocks. We also became members, entered the portfolio contest each year and built a lucrative portfolio.

We met once a month and each time someone wanted the club to consider a stock to purchase, they had to present the stock to the club, report on the company's five-year growth, their earnings per share, price to earnings ratio (PE ratio), revenue growth, profit margins, debt levels, cash flow, and market share. Additionally, the member would give us the ticker symbol, and present the company's highest price, lowest price and current price as of the day before. Once that information was presented and the members had a pretty good picture of the company, the group would discuss the company then vote on whether or not to purchase the stock. If there was a "yes" vote, then the treasurer would purchase the number of shares agreed upon. After five years, our portfolio had grown by 15%.

An Engineered Life

While registering at the ACI for airports international conference in Dallas, Texas, I realized there was a session that I wanted to attend for women in aviation. The breakfast started at 8:00a.m. and I realized that I only had five minutes to get there. While walking to the breakfast, I was lured by the shoe-shine couple to have my shoes shined. As I sat in the seat, I realized that getting my shoes shined at that time was not my priority. My priority was to arrive at the breakfast on time. I took the escalator upstairs and found a group of women who were also looking for the breakfast.

As we walked together, we realized that we were headed in the wrong direction, so we turned around and started heading back in the opposite direction. As we were going back, a lady was coming toward me who was also looking for the breakfast, so I told her to walk with us. We began chatting, soon to realize that she was the airport director for New York City Airport. At the time, they were embarking upon an $8 billion construction program. She and I had a great conversation and from that day, we formed a relationship, which turned into business opportunities. As a result of my connection with her, executives from New York City Airport flew down and gave presentations to our NABWIC members, resulting in billions of dollars of opportunities for our members to go after. As of today, they have made several presentations to NABWIC, many times via zoom meetings.

This is an example of an engineered life designed by God. He puts us in the right places at the right times to meet the right people. It is not always about us being blessed or on the receiving end of favor, but He will also place us in positions to be able to be a blessing to others, an answered prayer for them. This is how God, in His divine wisdom navigates our lives. We must continue moving forward and doing all that we can do while being willing to learn from the experiences and education that life brings, whether they're our own experiences or the experiences of others. The irony in this story is that, as the founder of the National Association of Black Women in Construction, one of my goals for the organization at the time was to form a chapter in New York City. Now, we have a strategic partner in the likes of the director of the airport for New York. Remember that it is God who engineers our circumstances and whatever they may be, we must see Him in them while continually abiding with Him, in, for, and through it all. Your engineered life will also include temptations, struggles, and challenges, but I am encouraged from the Word in Luke 22:28, *"You are those who have continued with me in my trials."* Be encouraged right now, even though the road maybe lonely. Watch God as He changes you and engineers your life through your circumstances.

Self-Education

Self-education is the process of obtaining knowledge, skills, and expertise on your own, without formal instruction or guidance from traditional institutions such as colleges or universities. Self-education involves you taking initiative and responsibility for your own learning, often through books, online courses, tutorials, videos, mentors, or hands-on experiences. Self-education allows you to pursue specific interests, tailor your learning pace, and explore diverse subjects. Self-education empowers you to continuously expand your knowledge and skills in a variety of areas instead of one main subject. Napoleon Hill said in 'Think and Grow Rich', the following as it relates to education: *"An educated man is not necessarily one who has an abundance of general or specialized knowledge. An educated man is one who has so developed the faculties of his mind that he may acquire anything he wants, or its equivalent, without violating the rights of others."* By this statement, Napoleon Hill knew that one could be self-educated. My self-education in the area of construction continued to increase my competence while building confidence as I continued to develop proficiency in construction. To augment what I was learning, I began to volunteer with Black contractors on the weekends. I did this so that I could apply the knowledge that I had gained. Unknowingly, these decisions were beginning to determine my destiny in construction as a lifelong career.

Formal Education

Formal education is often attained through college degrees or institutions and equips you with valuable knowledge and skills. However, the true value of this education lies not only in the acquisition but most importantly, in application. Some individuals, despite holding impressive degrees, still struggle to apply their knowledge in practical ways. This can happen for various reasons, such as a lack of motivation, limited real-world experiences, or a disconnect between theoretical learning and practical application. In those cases, their education may fail to translate into meaningful contributions to their careers or society. On the other hand, when people effectively apply their education, its value becomes evident and enables them to solve complex problems, innovate, and excel in their fields while becoming an asset to society. It is important to remember that having a degree does not make you intelligent and not having one does not make you dumb.

Education should be the bridge between theory and practice, which empowers you to lead a fulfilling life. Formal education, such colleges and universities, is not the path for everyone, and there are various alternative routes to becoming educated and still lead a successful life such as what has been explained in this chapter already. Other ways to education yourself includes vocational training, online learning, self-education, entrepreneurship, certifications, short courses, etc. The key is to cultivate a mindset of lifelong learning, which ensures continuous personal and professional growth. This involves seeking out knowledge and skills throughout your entire life because education is a life-long process. The minute you stop learning new things is the very minute that you get old.

Educational Balance

Educational balance is required for continuous learning regardless of how that education is acquired. Do you know anyone who is highly educated, but they don't do much to apply the education that they have obtained? They have college degrees but lack basic common sense. Or do you know the person who has too much education, has become so obsessed with gaining knowledge that they have become an educated fool? Some educated people forget how to apply their knowledge in practical situations and never find a way to use the knowledge to benefit themselves or others. These same individuals may have a plethora of diplomas, degrees, or certificates that they could plaster a wall with, yet at the same time, they are financially starving to death. Therefore knowledge, without application is useless. The bottom line is that education does not guarantee success. Only the application of the education will do that. Educational balance can also be obtained by diversifying your reading. It would be advantageous to balance your reading in the same way that you balance your diet.

Mastermind Readers

One thing that was and still is required of everyone in our mastermind group is to read at least one book a month. We all read the same book, then discussed it during the meetings. Understanding the value of books, we started off by reading those that were recommended by authors of other books. After each mastermind meeting, we talked about how the books impacted us and how we could apply the information into our individual lives. I could see how the information in those books motivated and changed the lives of the ladies in the mastermind group.

Car Exercises

Education was always pursued in the McNeill household. Before computers and audio recordings, there were always many educational materials and activities. For example, a dictionary, a newspaper, magazines, flashcards, an encyclopedia, a thesaurus, math workbooks, and other types of educational exercises in the back seat of my car for our daughters Danelle and Ionnie. As they grew older, we could see the benefit and value of those car exercises over the years. To this day, they each have a deep love for education and learning. Another exercise was reading street and highway signs, directional sights and/or airport signs. Each morning Ionnie would get the newspaper and read an article out loud. If she ran across a word in the article that she did not know, she would look it up using the dictionary in the back seat. She then would re-read the sentence with the word in it to understand what the sentence was saying. We would also do math exercises and other educational activities. This was an automatic practice that was done every time we got in the car while she was in elementary, middle and high school. I made sure that her mind stayed active. For me, next to God and my family, reading is one of the most important things to me. I can live without music, TV, social media, but I simply will not be content without reading. That is a non-negotiable for me. Wise men and women read. Studious people read. Gurus read. Experts in their fields read. What about you, do you read?

Builder's Toolbox 

- ❖ In what ways do you ensure that the knowledge you acquire has a purpose and aligns with your personal or professional goals?

- ❖ How do you plan to study and develop your passion and gift, that thing that you love to do?

- ❖ What steps are you taking to become the "go-to" person in your industry, and how do you assess your current level of expertise?

❖ How do you apply the concept of specialized knowledge to your career, and what niche have you developed or are developing?

❖ How do you balance formal education with self-education, and what role does each play in your lifelong learning journey?

You Must have a Dream!

What is your dream in the area of Education?
Write it down.

____

____

____

____

____

____

____

____

____

____

____

____

5

Personal Development

*The will to win, the desire to success, the urge to reach your full potential,
these are the keys that will unlock the door to your personal excellence.*
~Confucious

The first prerequisite for personal growth and development is to ask yourself questions starting with a personal assessment, which will be explained more in this chapter. How do you manage your personal life while juggling work and recreation, family and friends, mind, and body? This is answered through a personal development assessment. A research study by the Association of Executive Search Consultants indicated that 56% of business executives had not achieved work/life balance and 46% indicated that their work/life balance had declined within the past five years. Personal Development impacts your life in every way and in every area. I had been masterminding for many years before I realized that there was a need to envision what a personal development plan should look like for me. The answer came while having lunch with a very good friend, Dr. Tina Dupree, President and Founder of the Motivational Training Center (She is also known as "The chicken Lady.") Dr. Dupree is an expert in motivational programs, especially designed to inform, inspire, motivate and leave a lasting impression, with over twenty-five years of experience and author of five books, she is also a personal and professional development expert. We had agreed to go to lunch because I wanted to share with her how mastermind was impacting my life. At the time, the categories that we masterminded in were spiritual, financial, family, education, health, business, recreation, civic and creativity. Dr. Dupree asked me why there was no personal development category. She began to explain the need to develop personally and stated that speaking and writing would be good starting points.

Assessing Personal Development Skills

Personal development is a deeply personal journey, unique to each individual, and there's no one-size-fits-all approach to achieving it. After I added the personal development category as an area to set goals in, the desire to review, assess and enhance my skills in those areas grew. I also included branding and marketing to take me on a whole new journey. My personal introspection began to change as I started focusing on those areas in the personal development category. I began to search for those in my industry who I could model after and learn from. I also began to challenge myself to speak-to-share what I was learning and had already learned. Adding this category became a game-changer for me in my industry because I began to speak more professionally and expand my level of influence. Having personal development as a category to set goals in is crucial because it leads to a more balanced life. While work, finances, health, and the other areas are important, dedicating time to personal growth ensures that you do not neglect your well-being or overall life satisfaction. Although my focus was on improving my speaking, my career and business enhanced as well. The area of personal development also caused me to look around at the people who were closest to me to ascertain if they also had a desire to grow personally and expand their level of influence professionally. Doing this reminded me of something I once heard Bishop TD Jakes say, *"If you are the smartest person in your group, then you need a new group."* I was looking for those who were smarter than me.

A potential dream in the area of personal development for me, is created by admiring the lives of successful people. They do not have a "to do" list, but a "to be" list. For example, I want to be more generous, more patience, more learned, more reasoned. This requires me to develop personally. For me, this is a process of having quiet time, meditating, studying, writing, reading, and journaling, then, acting on the thought generated. The following quote stated by Martha Graham really made me think about fulfilling my uniqueness in a deliberate and goal-oriented way. *"You are unique and if that is not fulfilled, then something has been lost."* These words inspired me to focus on my uniqueness in the area of personal development. In assessing my personal development skills, I realized that my growth and development were in understanding that I must have a written plan to develop my skills and my uniqueness.

The Five-Hour Rule

Just as I discovered profound growth by setting intentional goals and assessing my skills, you too, can uncover a method that resonates with your needs and aspirations. One effective technique that has inspired countless high achievers is the Five-Hour Rule. This strategy offers a structured yet flexible way to prioritize deliberate learning and self-improvement. Whether you are seeking to refine your skills, expand your influence, or simply grow into the best version of yourself, the Five-Hour Rule provides a framework to ensure that you are consistently investing in your personal and professional growth. The term "Five-Hour Rule" was coined by entrepreneur Michael Simmons. He observed that many successful people consistently set aside time for deliberate learning, regardless of their busy schedules. He identified this practice across various high achievers and called it the "Five-Hour Rule," a personal development strategy where you dedicate at least one hour per day, or five hours a week, to deliberate and focused learning and self-improvement. This rule is used by successful people looking to achieve continuous growth. The key elements of the Five-Hour Rule include:

1. **Reading**: Engaging in reading to acquire new knowledge.

2. **Reflection**: Taking time to think about what has been learned in each day and how it applies to personal or professional life.

3. **Experimentation**: Applying new ideas and testing different approaches in work or daily life.

This practice helps ensure ongoing learning and skill enhancement, preventing stagnation in personal and professional development.

Cultivating Excellence as a Habit

As I continue to develop personally, I am reminded of the words of Aristotle, *"We are what we repeatedly do. Excellence then is not an act, but a habit."* I am therefore becoming more and more conscious of my daily habits, my hourly habits, my moment to moment habits; habits of thought and deeds. For example, in completing this book, I was in the habit of writing one page a day, then life happened, and I stopped writing. Regardless, the decision to write or not to write was a habit, not a habit of developing excellence or demonstrating commitment, but on the contrary. Life took over and the habit waned, for years and years and years. James Cleare in his book, 'Automatic Habits' encourages readers to rise to the occasion by using a two-minute rule in order to establish a habit before you can move on it. The two minute rule is breaking down a new habit into a two minute version to make them easier to start. But once you start, it is easier to keep going. For example, read one page each night before bed.

Iron Sharpens Iron

Iron sharpens iron, as one man sharpens another (Proverbs 27:17). Through the masterminding process, I am learning that this is the best way for me to grow in the area of personal development. The process of helping others improve in various areas of their lives encourages them to help me to grow in the many areas of my own life. After focusing on ways to improve myself personally, my new groups were formed by me inviting go-getters to start new mastermind groups of their own. As I began to grow professionally in the construction industry, I began to put on blinders as it related to race, color, and gender. My level of influence grew, causing me to learn new things from new colleagues and also enabled me to share things that I knew with them. I began to focus my attention on modeling prominent contractors in my industry and do some of the things they were doing. I soon discovered that most of them had contractor's licenses, so one of my personal, but also professional goals was to obtain my General Contractors (GC) license. I began sharing my goal of wanting to earn this license with my mastermind group. Each week, I would report that one of my goals was to obtain that GC license.

As years went on, I had been reporting the same goal with no progress made in that area until one day during a meeting, and after giving my mastermind report, one of the members said to me, *"I am so sick and tired of you saying that you are going to get your GC license each week. Tell us what you are willing to do to make that happen, please."* That remark was the kick-in-the-but that I needed to begin working on achieving that goal. I began preparing for the exam. Needless-to-say, I moved quickly because there was no way I was going to return to the group the next week without having taken some action towards making that goal a reality. I began to study, take prep courses, read books, and study the materials, etc. I even failed the exam a few times by only some points until the day came when I finally was able to report that I had passed the exam and obtained my General Contractor's license. The lesson learned was that writing down goals down is great, but there must be consistent action taken towards turning the goal into an achievement. A secondary lesson learned was that failure is not final as long as you learn from your mistakes and keep moving forward. I had failed the exam a few times, but eventually, I passed it and then helped four other individuals pass it on their first try. Now, I have two general contractor's licenses, a county one and a state one.

There is also another aspect of personal development which focuses primarily on the inner self. This aspect is the continuous process of improving yourself through things that enhance your skills, knowledge, and self-awareness, such as writing, speaking, taking a class, meditating, etc. This area also involves cultivating a positive attitude, watching your emotions, and strengthening self-discipline. By developing your inner self, you can prevent burnout, manage stress, and foster a well-rounded personality that enriches both personal and professional relationships. Personal development also enhances your self-awareness, which is crucial for strengthening emotional intelligence. Emotional intelligence involves recognizing and managing your emotions and understanding and influencing the emotions of others.

As we each grow personally, our ability to navigate emotional landscapes improves, leading to better decision-making, communication, and relationship-building. Personal development and emotional intelligence are closely related, with each reinforcing the other. Investing in yourself contributes to balance, self-awareness, and ultimately inner peace. As previously mentioned, an effective way to start your personal development journey is by taking a personal assessment. This involves asking specific questions about your strengths, weaknesses, goals, stress management, and areas needing improvement. Answering these questions provides insights into where your personal development efforts should be focused, creating a roadmap for growth and change. I have listed five reasons why personal development is important. Please take heed to the list and consider taking the area of personal development more seriously.

Focusing on personal development is crucial because it:

1. Enhances self-awareness and self-confidence.

2. Promotes a balanced life, ensuring that you do not neglect your personal well-being in favor of work or finances.

3. Improves emotional intelligence, enabling better management of your emotions and relationships.

4. Fosters resilience, adaptability, and the ability to overcome challenges.

5. Contributes to overall life satisfaction and fulfillment.

Maintaining balance in your life is extremely important because:

1. It prevents burnout and stress, which are common when you focus solely on work or finances.

2. A balanced life promotes mental and physical health, leading to longevity and happiness.

3. It allows for the development of a well-rounded personality, enriching personal and professional relationships.

4. Pursuing different interests and hobbies fosters creativity and innovation.

5. It ensures that your life is not one-dimensional but enriched with various experiences and skills.

A personal assessment can help identify areas needing improvement. Specific questions to consider in your assessment include:

1. What are my strengths and weaknesses?

2. What are my short-term and long-term goals?

3. How do I handle stress and setbacks?

4. What new skills or knowledge do I need to acquire?

5. How satisfied am I with my current life balance?

6. How strong is my relationship with those closest to me such as my spouse, my children and my siblings?

7. Am I self-disciplined? If so, in what areas?

8. What areas do I need more self-discipline in?

Answering these questions can highlight areas for growth, setting the stage for a focused personal development plan.

From Mediocrity to Improvement

My desire in this area of personal development is to steadily improve. Rarely do we move from mediocrity to excellence in one giant step. For me, this growth is incremental. We get there by making and taking numerous small steps. For example, I decided to journal daily after reading Julia Cameron's book, 'The Artist Way.' After years of journaling three pages per day, I began to notice that I used the word "today" in front of every entry. Eventually, I noticed that today's thoughts were my words, my quotes, my aha moments; so gradually, I began to share my thoughts on social media and called them #Thisisliving.

Later, I decided to publish my thoughts in a blog. After the blog, I published my thoughts in a daily journal, one thought per page as "thoughts to ponder". Then, from those small improvements, I began to make daily live streams. During Covid, I began to go live with my daily thoughts to encourage and inspire others by doing just a little daily. Every improvement in your life requires change, dedication and commitment, so start with just a little and be consistent because you can move from mediocrity to improvement, to excellence.

Mindset

What do you want? Have you ever had a desire, a need, a want for something that was not fulfilled in time?

Consider this quote:
The instinctive wants of the animal and the intellectual wants of Cuvier, the wants of nature and of the mind of Leverrier were alike, and thus the results; here the thoughts of an existence, there an

existence. A well-defined lawful want, therefore, furnishes the reason for the more complex operations of nature.

~Charles Haanel

The statement above says it all concerning our driving desire from nature to having a well-defined want. The more clearly we can see it in our imagination, the stronger will be the pull, the desire to be, to do, and to have the want. For example, for years in my construction company, my desire was to ensure that my employees were paid weekly. I needed a specific amount by a specific date each week and by some way, somehow, it was always achieved. I believed because it was well-defined. Knowing exactly what I wanted, developing a plan while praying, and planning that it would all work out was the fuel that contributed to my manifestations. This all depended on me grinding every day, working, calling, and asking as if it all depended on me and praying as if it all depended on God. My desire was achieved every single week for years, even until this very day. No longer a desperation, I began to learn to work on my mindset and to work "on" the business instead of "in" the business. The point here is that you must have a well-defined want.

A common denominator in successful leaders is that they have the habit of doing one small thing every day toward their ultimate end, their desire, their goals. They live with this mindset day in and day out. For example, professional bloggers, podcasters, and YouTubers share on social media as a habit on a daily basis. Charlie Monger and Warren Buffet do something every day in investing, Walt Disney with his imagination of what's possible, etc. These are all examples of successful leaders who had the habit of doing one small thing every day toward their ultimate goals. Since 2012, I started sharing something positive into the world on a daily basis and I continue to do this as of this writing. This focused energy draws the mind, resources, and people like a magnet in the achievement of that desire. Charles Haanel described in his book, 'The Master key System' how one's actions would help, *"As the eye seeks and receives satisfaction from colors, complementary to those which are given, so does need, want and desire in the largest sense induce, guide, and determine action."* In this quote, he is describing how actions in this statement helps to bring greater understanding of the Law of Inductive Reasoning in connection with the mindset required and actions which will bring forth that which we yearn for with a burning desire not just a mere want. In 'Think and Grow Rich' by Napolean Hill, there is a story about Edward C. Barnes' desire to work with Edison and the mindset which required him to persist and pursue with all diligence until he achieved his goal. Interestingly, seldom do we consider the fact that Edison also had a burning desire to find someone to sell his inventions to once they were created. Edison was the visionary, but Barnes was the integrator with the mindset to bring Edison's invention to light by giving them life through sales. *"When any object or purpose is clearly held in thought, it's precipitation and tangible and visible form is merely a question of time. The vision always precedes and itself determines the realization"* (Lilian Whiting).

It is important to manage your mind like you manage your time and your money. You must manage the mental traffic that cruises in your brain moment by moment. Optimists tend to live longer than pessimists. Pessimists do not let go of the past because of not being willing to forgive. Optimists realize that in order to protect their peace and to stay positive, they have to let things go, which in many instances means forgiving. I began to learn to move beyond my emotions as I continued to work on my mindset, especially through reading. I have learned and am still learning how to let those things go, past pain, hurt, betrayals and forgiving others regardless of fault, mine or others. I began to no longer dwell on my miseries or the miseries of others. I continued to make the choice to focus on a positive mental attitude regardless of the situation. My perspective and gratitude towards life, family, and business slowly transformed me into a more positive and loving person in spite of pain. In my daily journaling, I write down two to three things of gratitude and thankfulness.

I am learning especially from my construction experiences that personal growth challenges that come out of adversity often emerge opportunities to continue to grow abundantly. This is also substantiated in Rose Marie Rossett's quote, *"Adversity precedes growth."* The quote reminds me of the concept best illustrated by Koi Fish, *"If you put a Koi Fish in a fish bowl and give it food and water, it will never grow to more than two inches in size, but if you put it in a pond, it will grow to a foot in size."* The Koi Fish grows proportionately to the environment in which it lives. Think about it, when the Koi Fish is in the fishbowl, somebody is giving it food and water. It has no demands placed on it. It has no adversities, no challenges, no personal growth requirements. It is in a comfort zone. It is content. The moment you take the Koi Fish out of the fishbowl and put it in a pond, the water is deeper and colder. There are no boundaries. It takes more for the Koi Fish to survive. By necessity, it has to grow bigger and stronger so that it can deal with its environment. I am encouraged from this example of the Koi Fish to continue to grow through adversities and challenges.

Emotional Intelligence:

Personal development enhances self-awareness, and helps you understand your emotions, motivations, and behaviors. This self-awareness strengthens emotional intelligence. High emotional intelligence leads to better decision-making, improved relationships, and effective communication. Personal development and emotional intelligence are intertwined. As you grow spiritually, financially, educationally, and personally, your emotional intelligence also improves, leading to a more balanced, fulfilled, and successful life. Investing time in personal development is not just about achieving professional success but it is also about enriching all areas of your life, leading to a holistic well-being.

Self-Discipline

God designed life to be a discipline. Discipline comes through self-control. This means that we must work at controlling all negative elements that may rise up in us. However, before you can control conditions, you must control yourself, and self-mastery is the hardest job you will ever tackle. If you do not conquer self, you will be conquered by the elements outside of you. When you look into a mirror, you may see your best friend or your worst enemy. Self-discipline is a character trait that can be learned and nurtured through personal development. It involves consistently practicing self-control and gradually building habits that support disciplined behavior. Techniques such as setting clear goals, creating structured routines, and practicing mindfulness can help you enhance your self-discipline over time.

Self-discipline is a personal development trait that involves the consistent practice of self-control, self-regulation, and delayed gratification, enabling you to stay focused on your short and long-term goals despite temptations. Self-discipline is the foundation of your character because it determines what happens after you react. Having self-discipline helps you to stay committed to your goals, to wake up early, manage your time effectively, and maintain a positive disposition. Without self-discipline, it is challenging to achieve any form of lasting success because it is a continuing process that requires consistent effort and dedication. Discipline also plays a significant role in de-escalating conflicts. By maintaining control over your emotions and reactions during a conflict, you can respond to tense situations calmly and rationally, rather than impulsively. This can prevent misunderstandings and reduce the likelihood of conflicts escalating. For example, in a heated argument, a self-disciplined person might pause to listen and understand the other person's perspective instead of reacting defensively. *When you have learned to control yourself, you will have found the world within, which controls the world without.* (Charles Hannel)

When I know exactly what I want, my desire to do it is easier to accomplish with self-discipline. For example, each year, I set a goal to rise before 4:00a.m every morning, regardless of the time zone. This is without setting an alarm of any kind. The noise from the alarm puts me in a different kind of mood, which is not necessarily the best way for me to start my day. Over the years, I have learned that my body has an inborn alarm clock of its own. This clock is set the night before by drinking a glass of water before bed. This body clock always alarms before 4:00a.m. It quietly says, "I need to be relieved." Eventually, I must rise to go to the restroom. My next challenge comes in determining the next self-discipline I need to master after rising. These are the daily duties that determine my future and the intentions which are set forth at that moment, which sets my day into actions. Self-discipline enables me to meditate, read, pray, journal, drink water, take vitamins, and then exercise. This self-discipline gives me the best results for the moment, the hour, the day. This habit I call, "My daily date with myself" which I eventually published in a journal called, "My daily date with myself."

Lack of self-discipline can lead to a myriad of negative outcomes. It may result in poor split-second decision-making, procrastination, and failure to meet goals. This can further lead to a lack of progress in personal and professional life, decreased self-esteem, and strained relationships. In severe cases, it can contribute to unhealthy behaviors and lifestyle choices, such as poor diet, lack of exercise, and substance abuse. As I learned that each act of self-discipline in my life over time would strengthen every other act of self-discipline in my life, I decided to continue my exercises. I started with mind-strengthening activities. In strengthening my mind, I needed to find ways and means to do it by using specific strategies. For example, in 1980, when I decided to take the general contractor's exam, I had to become disciplined to study. The means and the messy middle was the studying part. However, I did not start studying for the exam until years later. Studying required a schedule. The schedule required self-discipline to do the work of setting and keeping the schedule seven days a week. Years later, after mastering self-discipline in this area, I was able to past the exam albeit after six attempts.

Daily I am tempted to not make my bed. The thought is that I can save time by skipping task. I can get to it later after I exercise. No-one will know or care. However, my daily self-discipline will begin right here. This small task of making my bed sets the tone for other self-disciplines with this diminutive act of making my bed immediately. The daily decision of committing to do a positive act continues with discipline starting with a small decision and a small discipline. The muscle, the practice, the daily discipline has helped me to manage big decisions. Another discipline that I decided to develop was to become a positive thinker. My actions to achieve this discipline was to start reading bestselling authors in the area of personal development and self-motivation. Reading authors such as Norman Vincent Peele, Og Mandino, and many others has helped me to achieve this goal. By reading motivational books, I began to have ideas which I have put into my daily journal. This encourages me to create the discipline to journal every day and to do the next best thing from small ideas, then the next best thing, then the next, then the next. I began to develop the discipline to study the things that I could do and to make changes in each area of my life and my businesses. I began to have the curiosity to find out how things work. For example, I wanted to learn how to invest. The discipline, motivation, and the mindset required led me to learn from the experiences of others by attending seminars and conferences while reading books on investing. This too, required self-discipline. This desire to want to do the work reminds me of a quote by Jim Roy, which says, *"Work harder on yourself than you do no your job."*

Investing time in ourselves begins by starting with a personal inventory. Personally, I have learned that my financial and personal success is directly related and connected to my personal inventory which requires personal improvement. Specifically working on myself includes defining and refining my niche and acquiring new skills and abilities to become a better person while answering the call of God upon my life. Personal development is the foundation and starting point for achieving your dreams, goals, and desires. The following are some of the personal development areas in my life, of which I have set specific goals over the years:

1. Spiritual
2. Family
3. Financial
4. Health
5. Education
6. Profession
7. Business
8. Recreation
9. Creativity
10. Civic

My desire is to encourage you to develop new skills, set specific goals, then decide to take action with your life plan in each of these ten areas. By documenting this process, it helps you to understand and see that small acts of self-discipline develops skills and increases confidence, character, and commitment in the achievement of your desires. Helbert Hubbard quoted the following, *"Self-discipline is the ability to make myself do what I should do when I should do it whether I feel like it or not."* This quote represents a deep understanding of self-discipline as a great virtue and attribute. "To do that which I know I should do whether I feel like it or not." This is my daily duty to discipline my mind, my body and my spirit and encompasses the process of learning what habit I must develop that works best for me. For example, the more I read about the benefits and internal power of learning more about my body, I better understand how to discipline it. This was important when starting with daily exercises. I have made exercise a priority upon rising within the first hour every morning no matter where I am in the world. While traveling to California or any other geographical location with a time zone different from mine, I will still rise at 5:00a.m although I may have arrived to that place at midnight. Upon rising, I will go directly to their gym. This self-discipline requires me to be mindful and to always pack my gym clothes when I travel. Doing this eradicates the excuse of not exercising. This same self-discipline is required for taking my vitamins, taking care of my skin, and drinking 64 ounces of water daily, all while making healthy food choices, even when in restaurants. When it comes to eating, self-discipline comes in when I choose a salad and a protein rather than a burger and fries. No matter how I may feel in my body, my mind and my spirit are always urging me to choose wisely, but only after it has been disciplined. I am learning that my mind and my body follow the thoughts from my spirit. So what comes first for you? Is it the chicken or the egg? Is it your mind or your body? I am reminded of 1st Corinthians 9:27 from the Amplified Bible, *But [like a boxer] I strictly discipline my body and make it my slave, so that, after I have preached [the gospel] to others, I myself will not somehow be disqualified [as unfit for service].*

How to Strengthen Self-Discipline

I have identified below, different techniques that you can use to strengthen self-discipline:

1. **Set Clear Goals**: Define specific, achievable goals and outline the steps needed to reach them.

2. **Create a Routine**: Establish a daily routine to build structure and consistency in your actions.

3. **Prioritize Tasks**: Focus on high-priority tasks first to ensure that your essential goals are met.

4. **Practice Mindfulness**: Engage in mindfulness or meditation practices to improve focus and emotional regulation.

5. **Self-Monitoring**: Keep track of your progress and hold yourself accountable for your actions.

6. **Reward Yourself**: Recognize and reward your achievements to stay motivated.

By consistently applying these strategies, you can develop and enhance your self-discipline, leading to greater success and fulfillment in various aspects of life.

BUILDER'S TOOLBOX 

* How well do I understand my inner self? What practices can I implement to deepen this understanding?

* How often do I reflect on my thoughts, emotions, and behaviors? What can I do to increase my self-awareness?

* How effectively do I manage my emotions in various situations? What strategies can I use to enhance my emotional intelligence?

* How disciplined am I in pursuing my goals? What areas of my life require more self-discipline?

* Are my personal development goals clear and achievable? How can I break them down into manageable steps?

* How open am I to receiving constructive feedback from others? How can I use this feedback to improve myself?

You Must have a Dream!

What is your dream in the area of your
Personal Development? Write it down.

6

Health

I have learned that success is to be measured not so much by the position that one has reached in life as by the obstacles which he has had to overcome while trying to succeed. ~Booker T. Washington

You must have a dream to have a dream come true to be health conscious. What is your dream for a healthy life? What does that look like for you? My vision in the area of health is for my body to function as optimally as possible until the day I transition out of this earth. Have you given thought to whether or not you will be healthy enough to live alone when you are 72, 82, or 92 years old? Will your children take you home with them or will they take you to a "home" or facility for the elderly? The mind-body connection became very apparent to me as our mastermind group began to read books in the area of health. One of the first books I read on health, which changed my total viewpoint on health and caused me to become more health conscious, was, 'Fit for Life' part 2 by Harvey and Marilyn Diamond. The idea that there is a deep connection between the mental, spiritual, and psychological that impacts one's physical health was new for me. Something as simple as positive daily thoughts, daily prayers, and meditation made a big difference in how I felt.

Mental Health

In the late 1970s, my mental state was not as positive as it could be for lack of understanding of how to direct my thinking, cultivate positive thoughts and recognize and dismiss negative ones.

I learned that there are two types of people that can impact your health, positive thinkers and negative thinkers. At the time, I was definitely a negative thinker, and it was impacting my health. My negativity was also affecting those around me. Prior to reading, Think and Grow Rich, I found myself in an emotionally bankrupt situation in most of the major areas of my life, including family, financial, work, and spiritual. All of these combined impacted my health in a negative way. The books, The Power of Positive Thinking and Think and Grow Rich had been recommended by my physician when I went to see him due to ill health. He felt that my health was related to my mind and psychological well-being, and he recommended reading to me. My health at that time was work-related, so I took his advice. As I read the book, and allowed the book to read me, I began to apply the principles of positive thinking. I began to see, feel, and believe by faith everything that I was reading. As I began to learn "how" to change negative thinking into positive thinking, positive results began to gradually manifest.

Prior to learning about the impact of positive thinking, I had been allowing my mind to be filled with negativity. I finally came to realize that as I continued to cling to negativity, it drew negative people, negative thoughts, and negative situations to me. However, as I began to see all things positively and began to learn how to make the mental switch in my mind by using scriptures and a new belief system that all things were working together for my good, the power of positive thinking helped me to approach the challenges of life with a positive attitude. In the past, my negative thinking and negative attitude had me constantly worrying about the challenges of life, but now, when faced with such challenges, I ask myself how I can make the best of the situation and work it out for my good, especially when in the service of others. As a result of changing my thought patterns, my health began to improve.

Physical Health

While reading Fit for Life, I began to learn a lot about the who, what, when, where, why and how of the human body. Of the many health books that I have read over the years, that one stands out at the very top in my memory because it immediately caused me to act. Harvey Diamond managed to explain the design and operation of the human body in a way that even a child could understand. The more I read, the better I understood the great manufacturing machine called the human body. I also better understood how the combination of foods consumed at certain times of day mixed with other foods could negatively impact the body. My body could only operate and manufacture on what I gave it, good food or bad food. I began to understand how the thoughts I think while eating impacted my health and my emotions as well.

I will admit that I did not want to know many of the truths about my favorite foods such as cereal and veal, but the Diamonds backed up their facts with over 500 scientific bibliography references, which helped to explain how each food category that I was eating impacted the manufacturing plant called my body. I also began to look at exercising differently. I began to walk more regularly for a minimum of 30 minutes a day and continued this exercise for many years even until this day. In addition, I started to visit my doctors more regularly to have my machinery checked out internally and externally. These visits included, but were not limited to, the podiatrist, the optometrist, the chiropractor, the cardiologist, etc. I also made sure that I had colonics, mammograms, pap smears, and regularly visited my general practitioner. For mental health, I visited the spa and got massages. Thomas Edison once said, *"To do much clear thinking, a man must arrange for regular periods of solitude when he can concentrate and indulge his imagination without distraction."* This is a simple, yet powerful and profound statement! A large part of our health comes from our feelings and mental health. For example, when you rise each day, do you check your mood? It may become a determining factor of how you will physically feel for the remainder of the day.

As humans, the first thing we do after waking up is to go to the bathroom to relieve ourselves physically, but how do you release yourself spiritually, mentally, and emotionally? Julia Cameron, author of the book, The Artists Way, suggests that we journal and write three morning pages of whatever is on the mind. There can be many causes of imbalance in the area health. One main cause is the lack of knowledge in the areas regarding food, exercise, water, and nutrition. Brenda Jaeck, a certified meditation and lifestyle coach states that, *"Incorrect food choices, lack of sleep and exercise, stress, troubled relationships and more can cause imbalance in the body."* When you have no time to eat correctly, no time to process thoughts and no time to rid your mind of constant chatter, the body becomes imbalanced. Finding balance in your health is a journey. My suggestion in this area is to create a health plan for yourself and mastermind your health goals with your mastermind group. Life Lessons in the area of health is teaching me that the more I read and learn about health, the more informed I am of how to change my health habits. Examine your life's priorities around your health while creating a plan of action and implement the plan regarding daily dietary needs and daily exercise.

Early Rising

A major part of your mental health that can impact you positively is to become a habitual early riser. There was a time when I would constantly wake up late, leave the house late, and arrive to my destination late. I would then rush through my whole day, stressed and pressed and always trying to catch up. This began to wear on my health negatively, affecting me mentally and also physically. However, after analyzing each area of my life and reading Fit for Life, I now get up each morning by 4:30a.m and I have a date with myself consisting of prayer, meditation, journaling and reading. Journaling is a wonderful stress-reliver. It is a great outlet of expression and a wonderful day to start the day. During this date with myself, I also take my vitamins, stretch, exercise, eat fruit and prepare for a healthy day. I have been doing this since 1985. Rising early has so many benefits. It lays the foundation for your day, keeps you calm, stress-free and provides mental clarity.

This process of understanding the connection between mind, body and spirit all started with becoming health conscious. Becoming health conscious for me, simply means to think about health during the day, be conscious of what I eat, starting with fruit in the mornings on an empty stomach, salad and protein for lunch, and a light dinner. As a part of being health conscious, I am constantly reminded to read something about health on a weekly basis. As you begin to understand more about health and seek to become more attuned to things that may contribute negatively to your health, consider answering the following questions:

- Is your workload stressing you out?
- Do you drag yourself home at the end of the day?
- Do you have a hard time getting up in the mornings?
- Are you overweight?
- Are you frequently tired, frazzled, or have bad moods?
- Do you have poor sleeping habits?
- Do you exercise regularly?
- Are you under the weather a lot or often don't' feel your best?
- Do you take the time to focus on specific health areas in your life?
- Do you read books on health?
- Do you drink 64 ounces of water daily?

If the honest answers you gave were not favorable, then there needs to be a change. It doesn't matter how much money you make, how powerful you are, what your position or title is, or how much influence you have, if you don't have good health, then none of that is worth a hill of beans. How are you enhancing your energy and strengthening your heart rate? How are you increasing your cardiovascular health? You only have one body and how you treat it will determine how it treats you. The following books have been very helpful to me in this area. One is entitled, 'You the Owner's Manual' by Michael F. Roizen and the other one is, 'You're not Sick, You're Thirsty' written by Fereydoon Batmanghelidj.

Your Health is Your Wealth

Without health, nothing matters. If you are not able to walk, feed yourself, dress yourself or wash yourself, then what good would it be to have lots of money, a nice home, a fancy car, and nice clothes? Without good health, none of those things matter. If you have no energy to put your hand to your mouth to eat, then what does acquiring success in all of the other areas discussed matter? What is the purpose of acquiring material goods if you cannot enjoy them? Maintaining good health should be at the top of your priority list after God. If you are good to your body, your body will be good to you. In the list below, I have identified some areas of health to consider incorporating into your lifestyle. They are in no particular order, but I would like you to consider each area as a priority for good health:

Spiritual Health

Having a relationship with God through prayer is one way of releasing what is on your heart and mind. Giving thanks to your creator, then offering your supplication to Him can give you peace and is a great way to start the day. Releasing your heart to the Lord can increase your health. We don't get ulcers by what we eat. We get ulcers by what eating us.

Rest

Rest and sleep are not the same, but they both are important. To rest, is to slow down and recover from all activities, including mental activities and allow the body to recuperate from stress and fatigue. You cannot continue going and going and going like the energizer bunny. You must slow down and take some time to rest. As I age, I find myself making time to rest more. For example, I drive an electric car, which requires charging during the day. Therefore, when I stop to recharge my car, which is usually in the afternoons, I will also stop to recharge my body by taking a nap. I turn up the AC, turn off my cellphone and recline my seat as I put on the timer set for 15-20 minutes. At the end, the car is charged and so am I.

Sleep

You must get some good sleep. A good night's sleep is crucial for cognitive function, and emotional regulation. It is essential for overall well-being, restoring energy, and maintaining optimal performance in daily activities. Continuing to deprive yourself of sleep can lead to a range of health problems. A good night's sleep is critical for the body's physical and mental functioning.

Food

Eating the right foods is essential for maintaining good health because it provides the body with essential nutrients, vitamins, and minerals required for overall well-being. A balanced diet supports a healthy immune system and reduces the risk of chronic diseases such as heart disease and diabetes. Nutrient-rich foods also support brain function and aid in digestion. Poor dietary choices can lead to illnesses. I encourage you to read the book, Fit for Life that I talked about in this chapter as well as other books that promote good health.

Mental Health

Your mental health is a significant component of your overall health because it impacts your emotional, psychological, and social well-being. Your mental health influences how you think, feel, act, and affects your ability to cope with stress, maintain relationships, and make choices. On the contrary, poor mental health can lead to mood disorders, anxiety, and impaired functioning. Recognizing and addressing mental health concerns is essential for achieving and sustaining a holistic state of well-being because your mental and physical health are interconnected. For example, my mental health and my spirit are invigorated by reading and listening daily to motivational and educational information, such as a Proverb a day on YouTube and reciting the self-confidence formula from the book, 'Think and Grow Rich'.

Loving Relationships

Loving relationships have greatly affects your overall health. Positive relationships provide emotional support, reduce stress, and promote feelings of happiness and security. Loneliness and isolation have been linked to various health issues. Loving relationships play a crucial role in enhancing mental and physical well-being, contributing to a longer, healthier life. Stay away from drama and conflict. Cultivate love, laughter, and joy!

Exercise

Engaging in a little exercise each day has a significant positive impact on your overall health. Even a small amount of physical activity can improve cardiovascular health, increase muscle strength, and enhance flexibility. Exercise helps control body weight, regulate blood sugar levels, and reduce the risk of chronic diseases such as heart disease and diabetes. Regular exercise also enhances your mood, reduces stress, and promotes better sleep. If you do not exercise, then consider starting to do a little something such as walking for 30 minutes each day.

Water

Drinking lots of water is extremely important for overall health. You must have adequate hydration because it improves and maintains digestion and helps transport nutrients. Water also flushes out waste products and lubricates your joints. Drinking plenty of water also supports optimal kidney and urinary function as well as promotes healthy skin. It has also been proven that drinking plenty of water can improve cognitive function and mood. Water is crucial for maintaining optimal physical and mental well-being.

Sunshine

Getting natural sunshine has several positive effects on your health. Sunlight exposure helps the body produce vitamin D which is essential for strong bones, immune function, and mood regulation. Sunlight also boosts serotonin production which lifts the mood. Even a moderate amount of sun exposure can lower blood pressure and support cardiovascular health. However, excessive sun exposure can lead to skin damage and increase the risk of skin cancer, so it is essential to strike a balance and use sun protection when necessary. In moderation, natural sunshine contributes to better physical and mental well-being.

Air

Exposure to natural environments and fresh air has been linked to reduced stress, better immune function, and enhanced well-being. Natural air, free from pollutants and filled with oxygen, also has a profound positive impact on your health. Breathing in clean air supports lung function and enhances overall cardiovascular health. Clean air can improve energy levels, mental clarity, and mood by increasing your brain's supply of oxygen. Polluted air can lead to respiratory problems and other health issues. Prioritizing access to clean, natural air is essential for maintaining optimal physical and mental health.

Intellectual Health

Stimulating your mind, which is also known as your intellectual health by engaging in mentally challenging activities such as reading, self-education, and continuous learning is essential for your overall well-being. Intellectual stimulation helps maintain cognitive function, memory, and problem-solving abilities. Intellectual stimulation can also lower the risk of age-related cognitive decline and conditions such as Alzheimer's disease. By keeping the mind active and engaged, intellectual health supports overall mental and emotional well-being and can foster a higher quality of life throughout one's lifespan.

BUILDERS TOOLBOX 

- ❖ In what ways do you recognize and address the connection between your mental, spiritual, and physical health in your daily life?

- ❖ How regularly do you engage in physical exercise, and have you incorporated walking or other forms of exercise into your daily routine?

- ❖ How often do you visit the doctor for regular check-ups, including visits to specialists such as podiatrists, optometrists, and cardiologists?

- ❖ What strategies do you use to manage stress, and how effective have they been in improving your mental and physical health?

- ❖ Do you have a morning routine that includes activities such as prayer, meditation, journaling, and exercise to set a positive tone for your day?

- ❖ How much attention do you pay to your hydration and nutritional needs, and do you make conscious choices to drink plenty of water and eat nutrient-rich foods?

- ❖ Do you incorporate practices such as getting adequate sleep, spending time in nature, and ensuring you get sunlight and fresh air into your health regimen?

You Must have a Dream!

What is your dream in the area of your
Health? Write it down.

7

Business

To be trusted is a greater compliment than being loved.
~George MacDonald

You must have a dream to have a dream come true in the area of business. when you are destined as an entrepreneur, it is in your blood. When you begin to realize that you were created to be a business owner, you may not know what that business is at first, but in your quest to find out where you belong in the world of entrepreneurship, you may try many different things. On this journey, you will have some failures, you may lose large amounts of money, and experience great disappointments, but with determination and persistence, you will find your niche; you will find where you fit; and you will find that thing that has been waiting for you to claim it. Until such time however, you must try as hard as you can to be wise and listen to that inner small voice that leads and guides you. It is God, but some call it intuition. Many call it "women's intuition", but not only women have it. Men have it as well. When you refuse to listen to that still small voice, God, in His grace and mercy will send someone to warn you of impending dangers and/or failures that lie ahead.

My mother was a housekeeper, and my father was a gardener and entrepreneur. Growing up, my family did not have a lot of money, but my father was a dreamer and had an entrepreneurial spirit. My mother was a woman of great faith, and she instilled in us a deep sense of faith, prayer, love for God, and belief that I could have anything I wanted and be anything I wanted to be. Fortunately for me, I believed it. In my early adult life, I tried my hand in many ventures and made financial investments in all of them.

That Still Small Voice

If you are a believer, then praying and asking for God's guidance is essential before making financial business decisions, especially in business. I have had my share of both losses and wins in business. The times that I took heed to His still small voice, I was safe, but those other times when I didn't, failure and disappointed waited for me. In 1976, God's providence interceded for me in a business deal that I wanted so bad. There was a certain nightclub that I wanted to own. I had done my research and knew that the money-making potential was great. The owners wanted $100,000 for it. My husband and I had already invested $95,000 and we only needed $5,000 to close the deal, but we didn't know how or where we were going to get that remaining $5,000. I had liquidated almost everything I had to get the $95,000 and there was nothing else to liquidate. I had maxed out all of my credit cards and the only person I knew who had the money was my dad. I had been asking and pleading with him to loan me the money for that night club. He was adamantly against it and tried his best to talk me out of it. He said that he had tried that kind of business before, and it was not the kind of business that I should get into. He tried to give me the wisdom learned from his mistakes in that business. He told me that kind of business was not for me, and he did not have a good feeling about it in his spirit. For months he refused to give me the money, but I kept asking. This one particular Sunday, I told myself that I was going to ask him one last time and do my best to persuade him. While at my parents' home, my dad and I had a really good bonding time together. We talked and laughed. I shared things with him, we cried together, and the time we had was so precious that I at that moment,

I did not care if he gave me the money or not. I just enjoyed that time with him. I must've been there with him for about nine hours before leaving.

A $5,000 Life's Lesson

The next day, out of the blue, my mother called me and said, *"Your father has changed his mind. He is going to give you the money for the nightclub."* I was so shocked and immediately, I made arrangements to close the deal on the nightclub the next day. We went to my parents' house, picked up the money, and went to the nightclub. My attorney met me there, and I had the $5,000 in cash. The club owners, myself, and my attorney were in the middle of closing the deal when the phone rang. One of the owners said, *"Mrs. McNeill, it is for you."* Me, looking confused, took the phone. It was my mother. She said, *"You need to get here right away. Something has happened to your father."* I returned to the room where we were meeting, slid all of that money that was laid out on the table onto my dress, cuffed the front of my dress and ran out of there in haste. I reached home in time to see medics taking my father from the front lawn to the back of an ambulance on a stretcher. As I looked into his face. I saw no life. He was pronounced dead at the hospital that day. I found out from my mother that the money that he gave me, was money he had been saving all his life for his burial. I believe that he died spiritually, the moment he gave me that money. He had given it to me against his better judgment and made a decision contrary to his intuition. He gave the money to me, but in reality, he took it back. That $5,000 was used for his burial and from that day on, I never stepped foot into that nightclub again. He instinctively knew that that business was not for me, and he was going to stop me from going that route one way or the other. When we ignore the still small voice of wisdom speaking to us, God sends other voices. In this case, it was my earthly Father's voice, but I refused to listen. Since then, I am listening to that still, small Voice from my heavenly Father and my actions and business decisions are led by it. That

Voice never steers me wrong, but I had many, many more business lessons to learn.

The Amway Business

During the 1970s, while on my search for financial freedom, I was approached by many enthusiastic people to explore business opportunities with the Amway Corporation. It was not appealing at first, but after reading the first chapter in Think and Grow Rich where it outlined the six ways to turn desires into gold, I recognized the Amway business as an opportunity to help free me from debt, so when the next person asked me to look at it, I did. The Amway business taught me how to dream big and how to remove self-imposed limitations from my mind regarding finances and life as a whole. This was taught by transforming the mind through the use of a personal development system consisting of books, cassette tapes (yes cassette tapes) and seminars, to increase one's vision and teach them how to dream big. One of the big visions I had for myself, and our family was that of living in a beautiful home with sliding glass doors overlooking a pool on a golf course. I had cut out and placed a picture of this home on my refrigerator some years prior.

I had learned through the Amway personal development system, to program my subconscious mind to attract to me whatever it was that I desired, so I did just that. The Amway business was one of the best personal growth and development opportunities of my life because of the application of the principles they taught. Those principles did not only help in business, but they helped to build the man or woman of the business. Their essential goal was that if you build the person, the person will build the business. My entrepreneur endeavors since 1980, covered a wide range of business pursuits including a restaurant, a bar, retail, concessions, rental properties, multi-level marketing, and many, many other companies which I had started over the years. Some were successful, some not so much, but they each were building blocks and steppingstones towards my purpose and dream.

Seeds Planted

As I continued to learn more about entrepreneurship, I learned how to sell, starting with myself, then the products and services I was marketing at the time. The main concept I sold was "me, the corporation" a concept of personal growth and development through personal achievement. As I learned in Amway, they grew the person and the person in turn, grew the business. I gave books away and shared the weekly cassettes that we were required to listen to. I also encouraged people to attend personal development events with me. As a part of my personal development and continuous education, a desire to become a certified license general contractor emerged, so I went to a trade school to learn how to build a house from the ground up. I learned about construction and at the time, I was the only woman in the classes. While in trade school, I learned how to do most of the trades. I also learned that I could hire workers as subcontractors in every trade that was required. I also learned that many people who knew the trades, did not know the business, and many who knew the business, did not necessarily know the trades. For me, although I had learned the trade side, I had not yet learned the operation side of a construction company.

Preparation & Training

As a result of reading the story of Edison and Barnes, in the book, Think and Grow Rich, I was willing to take more entrepreneurial chances and low-paying job opportunities in exchange for experience. Shortly after finishing trade school, the Miami race riot happened in 1980 following the acquittal of four police officers in the death of Arthur McDuffie. After the riots, I came to Miami to help with the rebuilding because they were looking for contractors. As I would meet various Black contractors at those meetings, I would ask them if they needed volunteers. Business owners were glad to have a free laborer and I was more than happy to volunteer so that I could continue learning. Since I had learned so much in trade school, I had no problem doing roofing, carpentry, ordering materials, digging trenches, dry wall, painting, or helping with paperwork, etc. However, I did not have the application for connecting the book knowledge to the field knowledge. I volunteered for about three years, and it proved to be extremely beneficial because I learned so much. I also found out about the work habits of others. I would observe how folks would get paid on Friday, then not come to work on Saturday. Oftentimes, the companies would take any able body who needed some quick money to work. Finding good workers was a challenge for most construction companies. While volunteering, I would continue going to the meetings to find out about updates. While at one of the meetings one day, I found out that Mr. Thacker, from Thacker Construction was looking for someone to manage his construction office. I jumped at the opportunity to work for him because I thought in my mind that I could learn how to manage a construction company under him. While working for him, I learned everything I could. I became his protégé and he became my mentor. From the onset, I told Mr. Thacker that I eventually wanted my own construction company, but that I did not know about the operational side of it. Working with him would give me the experience I needed and teach me the things I needed to know about the business side. While working at Thacker Construction, I also began studying for my contractor's license.

MCO Construction

I started MCO Construction in 1982, almost 42 years ago (as of this writing) in Miami, Florida. It was my husband who planted the seed in me to start a construction company. As we were relaxing and talking one day in 1979, he said: *"If I had to do it all over again, I would not go to college. I would start a construction company."* My husband's words resonated with me because I had always wanted to start my own business. During this time, my husband and I were already investing in real estate. We owned our house, a house across the street from us, a duplex down the street, and one around the corner. When repairs were needed in our properties, we would go to the local library and conduct research on how to do the repairs and then would fix them ourselves. As we continued to read and do research, we discovered that construction workers made more money in an hour than we made in a day, and they sometimes made more in a day than we made in a week. That was the time that I decided to go to trade school to study and learn about how to build houses. Eventually, I started MCO Construction, but under someone else's license. However, I was still working as an office manager for Thacker Construction. I had read Think & Grow Rich, which had a deep impact on me, and I was motivated more than ever to start my own business. I had learned under Mr. Thacker that I needed to have a technical certification. Additionally, he told me that I needed to get a good estimator, a good CPA, a good banker, a good lawyer, and a good bonding company.

The first bonding company was referred to me by the county. Coincidentally, the company they referred to me was the company that had given Mr. Thacker his first bond. They respected him, his business acumen, and they had a high level of respect for him, so when they found out that I worked for him, they backed me more than the average small business, which enabled me to go after projects under $500,000, but over $200,00. Because of this, I did not have the competition that other small businesses had because other Black contractors were not able to bond over a certain amount. They were able to go after projects under $200,000 because anything under $200,000 did not need to be bonded, but they faced challenges with getting bonded for anything over that amount. Since I had the backing of the bond company, I was going after contracts left and right and was actually getting them.

I started MCO while continuing to work for Mr. Thacker and I did not stop working for Thacker Construction until he died some years later. After that, my only job was working at my own business, MCO Construction. After Mr. Thacker passed away, his business closed down, and I never worked for anyone else again. I had no choice but to put my heart, mind, and soul into my own business. After four years, I was able to double the salary that I was making at Thacker Construction in my company. I learned from my mentor that I needed a really good estimator, someone who gives you an estimate of how much it will cost to do the work, and I had a good one who knew the business of construction. My estimator taught me how to look for projects by going to the county, which had public bids, because legally, they had to advertise. Back then, everything was all on paper, so I would find projects, bid on them, and would win most of them. As a woman in a predominately male industry, it has not always been easy, but it has definitely been worth it.

The Little Yellow Card

When I was growing up in Palm Beach County in the 1960s, it was during the time of segregation. As a Black person, you could not travel to certain areas of town unless you had a little yellow card given by the police department verifying that you had permission to be in that particular (White part of) town after dark. The card was known as a work permit and was given regardless of age. Every Black person working in those areas had to have one. Fast forward to 1992, as a construction contractor in the same county, I bid and won a 20-million-dollar construction project to build the city of West Palm Beach's new police station. Prior to the award, I had spent 15 years traveling from West Palm Beach to Miami every day just to go to work in the construction industry because I was unable to work in my own hometown of West Palm Beach for three reasons: I was Black, I was female, and I was financially disadvantaged. Despite these obstacles, I was always looking for an opportunity to return home to work. So when the opportunity presented itself for the City of West Palm Beach to build a new police station for 20 million dollars, I realized for the first time in 15 years of commuting to Miami every day, that God was preparing me for such a time as that. I was reminded of the story of Joseph going from the pit to Potiphar's house, and to the prison to the palace, in order to prepare a place for his family.

Business Obstacles

Owning a business was not always easy and I ran into some hard times. There were obstacles, but my commitment to my team, my clients, and myself is what kept me in business for so many years. There were days that I did not have enough cash flow, but there were always creative ways to overcome those cash flow challenges. One creative way was to ask the owners to pay me in advance. Another creative way was to ask for checks payable to both parties, to me and whoever I owed. That would guarantee payment for them. Doing this also helped with not needing a bond. The reason for a bond is to ensure that the people will get paid. Success in construction was realized as a result of more than hard work. The principles that I am learning from Think and Grow Rich were followed diligently. The other contribution to my success in business was accountability that was reinforced through the process of masterminding. I founded the International Mastermind Association (IMA), starting with one group and expanding to groups all over the country. Accountability, the key to setting and reaching goals, was provided through the process of masterminding. I am also the founder of National Association of Black Women in Construction (NABWIC). I created a place for Black women and girls at all levels to connect in order to build a pipeline into the construction industry. This was a way of sharing my success. The association was created for four subgroups:

1. Black girls in junior high school, high school, and college. They could see themselves through us as entrepreneurs, architects, lawyers, contractors, laborers, small businesspeople, and other trades.

2. Black women in professions throughout corporate America. They control procurement and construction contract opportunities.

3. Black Women in the public sector: cities, counties, states, and school boards. They control procurement opportunities.

4. Black Businesswomen: business owners, those in the trades working as architects, engineers, and contractors.

Using the principles of Think and Grow Rich as a foundation, I have been able to create a mindset shift of what is possible, not just for myself, but for so many others. That has been and is still my vision. Closely following the principles of Think and Grow Rich has empowered me to build lives, families, and communities. As a master builder, it is my goal to build stronger and better lives, especially in the construction industry. You can do the same. Step out on faith and just do it! Develop the mindset, faith and belief that you can!

Every year in business you should take time to review, receive, replenish, restore, reassess, and then relax. Many of us spend more time and money planning our relaxing time for our vacation than we do planning our business time. Take time right now and do an assessment and a professional review of your business, your mindset, and your skillset. If you have ever read the book Acres of Diamonds by Russell Cromwell, then you know that some of the finest gemstones in business are in your own backyard, but you will only discover them if you take the time to review, receive, replenish, reassess, and restore your business. Begin now, to set the goals to take small steps to improve the quality of your business. Start with short-term goals for the next three to six months. Then you can look out at one year to five years, then to ten, etc.

Stay Relevant

Relevance and business are about staying connected to business contacts, unique, and valued in various aspects of life, and it is cultivated through self-awareness, active engagement, and continuous improvement. For you to be relevant means that you stay significant and valued in your social and professional circles. In your industry, being relevant involves standing out and being unique, which can be achieved through innovation, expertise, having a social media presence, and being a constant contributor to your field or industry by adding value. This uniqueness helps in establishing a distinctive presence that draws attention and respect. The reason why I said that social media plays a crucial role in maintaining or enhancing your relevance is because it provides a platform for you to share your ideas, showcase your expertise, and engage with a broader audience.

Staying relevant gives you a competitive advantage meaning that you stay useful, innovative, and up with the times. A relevant business is one whose name is associated with what they do. When you think of basketball, you think of Lebron James. When you think of top-of-the-line watches, you think of Rolexes. When you think of the lead in the computer industry, you think of Bill Gates. When you think of the innovator in social media, you think of Mark Zuckerberg. I can go on and on, but I think you get the message. What do people think of when they hear your name or your business' name? Losing relevance will ultimately cost you. Are you relevant?

We are immersed in a technological advanced digital society where social media plays a huge part in one's image and brand. By effectively using social media, you are able to amplify your voice, stay updated with industry trends, and connect with like-minded professionals and clients in your industry, thereby enhancing your relevance. The value that you place on yourself also contributes to your relevance. When you recognize their worth and capabilities, you are able to project confidence and authority, making you more compelling and influential. If you desire to be relevant in your market, then penetrate that market by engaging, inspiring, and influencing your market in a variety of ways, including social media.

One way that I stay relevant is to align myself constantly with industry leadership in my professional associations, industry associations, and civic associations. I am connected to over 50 such associations related to my life and my businesses. For example, construction associations include, but are not limited to Associated Builders and Contractors, Association of General Contractors, National Association of Women in Construction, and Association of Professional Estimators. In addition, industry associations include Association of Minorities and Airports, Conference of Minority Transportation Officials and Floridians for Better Transportation. These numerous associations include the following industries: water, energy, port, transportation, facilities, healthcare, and aerospace, just to name a few.

Advice to Aspiring Entrepreneurs

To date, I can truly say that the greatest sale I have ever made as a businessperson was the day I personally bought what I was selling. This was the day I saw the big picture. That was the day I truly began believing what I was doing to help my clients. When starting your business, make sure that your vision is crystal clear to you. Having a clear purpose is essential and makes it easier to embrace the business idea that God has given you. It is very sad that there are men and women who think they have failed when they don't succeed. Failure is only temporary, and if you are able to look beyond the temporary defeat and forge ahead in spite of obstacles, you will eventually experience the success from your hard work. However, if you give up after temporary defeat, you will never discover the success that awaited you just around the corner. Don't give up! Consider this, you are in five different businesses as an entrepreneur.

The First is the business of your craft. This is your skillset and your profession.

The Second is the business of the operation of the business of your craft, i.e. business development, payroll, human resources, invoicing, etc.

The Third is the business of relationships in learning how to turn contacts into contracts.

The Fourth is the business of your industry associations. You must be involved in at least one association related to your craft.

The Fifth is the business of money. This includes saving and maxing out your retirement account each year. We are taught how to make the money, but we are not taught how to make the money make money.

My advice to aspiring entrepreneurs is to focus on the five businesses that you are in in order to add value and increase profit.

Never Waiver

Since the start of MCO construction, I have never wavered in my decision to stay the course in providing the best value to all clients, both internal and external. Internal clients represent your team members and your employees in providing benefits and payroll. I have never missed making payroll to my clients, even though the road has not only been rocky and hard, but sometimes, there was no road at all. For example, when I started the business, we focused on very, very small projects and we financed the work by requesting mobilization (money from the client) because I was never able to borrow money because my credit was so bad. But as we grew from paying two-three payrolls per week to laborers, we grew to hiring 70-80 workers per week to then working in multiple trades. We never missed a payroll and I never wavered in my commitment to my team. There were many Fridays that I did not know where the money for payroll would come from, but I never wavered in my commitment. I became very creative during these times because I was unable to borrow money from the traditional bank. Imagine going from a $1,000 payroll for employees per week to paying 70-80 thousand dollars in payroll per week, but again, I never wavered! During these times, I found my God and I continued to learn what He not only could do but would do. I worked like it all depended on me and had faith like it all depended on God. I never wavered in my faith and trusted Him that all things were still working for my good.

BUILDERS TOOLBOX 

- ❖ Do you have a solid business plan for how you will lay the foundation for your business?

- ❖ Do you have mentors in the same industry to guide and help you navigate pitfalls in the business?

- ❖ Do you have a competitive advantage to help you stand out in your industry?

- ❖ Are you surrounded by capable and competent people that you can trust to do things when you are busy doing other things for the business?

- ❖ Are you constantly educating yourself on new innovations and changes in your field?

You Must have a Dream!

What is your dream in the area of your Business? Write it down.

8
Civics

Y ou must have a dream to have a dream come true in the civic area of your life. The biblical adage, *"It is better to give than to receive"* is very true from a civic standpoint. It is never too late to begin to give at least 1/3 of your resources towards services and causes that are aligned to your values, your dreams, and your desires. When you are civic-minded, you are constantly looking for ways to improve the world and for ways to attract the support of people who will help you to achieve your civic dreams. For example, early in my construction career, as an entrepreneur, I began to get involved in civic organizations and I started volunteering with others in the community because I observed positive role models who were also entrepreneurs doing the same thing. Those individuals were community-minded. Slowly, I began to observe the connection between the service they gave and the positive impact that it had on their businesses and also their lives. I began to create ways to align with organizations such as the various chambers of commerce. I never realized that every city, county, and state had a chamber for business connections. Every ethnic group also had a chamber for business connections. As I visited the various chambers, I saw the different ways in which I can serve my community. Eventually, I began to connect with entrepreneurs who were in the construction industry. That is when I noticed a void. There were not very many people who looked like me. This was the beginning of an idea to serve my own community in a civic way, as I watched others serve and build their own communities in similar civic ways. This desire to serve, gave me the impetus to create a local Black contractors' association which led to the formation of the National Association of Black Woman in Construction (NABWIC). As of this writing (2025), we are represented in twenty cities in the United States and still we are still growing.

Civic engagement, as I am learning, includes organizing, participating in associations such as rotary clubs, lions' clubs, Parent Teacher Associations (PTAs), boys' and girls' clubs, and many others. The importance of civic engagement is that the more we get to know and connect with others, the more we learn about the causes that are important to them and why those causes resonate deeply with them. This is when we are able to learn about people on an individual level. Doing this from an authentic place, knocks down the barriers of race, political affiliations, genders and religious backgrounds that sometimes separates us and connects us to a sense of service. This is what creates bonds and connections, which sometimes leads to business, which can turn into contracts, because it is evident that people do business with those they know, like and trust. I believe the aspirational sense to serve is the core that connects us and helps us to better understand the importance of making a difference as a fundamental way of life. Eventually, we begin to stop complaining about the problems when we realize through serving, that we have the ability and the capacity to do something about it.

You may not have ever thought about this, but you can also have a dream in the area of civics. What exactly does this mean you ask? From the standpoint of goal setting, civics refers to your rights and duties of citizenship. It involves understanding how the government functions from a local, state and national level, your understanding as a citizen in shaping public policy, joining organizations that are positively impactful to the community and social justice, and participation in democratic processes. As a citizen, you must be involved in activities such as voting, staying informed about current events, attending public meetings, and advocating for causes that benefit the community. Your involvement ensures that you contribute to the advancement of society and the effective functioning of democracy.

When I was a child growing up in Rivera Beach Florida, my father L.C. Cobb would encourage and almost admonish me to stay home more, but I wanted to visit my friends every chance I got. From sunup to sundown, I was gone. Again and again, he would say, *"Ann, why don't you stay home some and let your friends visit you. They can never visit you if you are always at their homes."* Over 30 years later, I finally began to understand what he meant after applying his advice to my business affairs. Let me explain. As part of my civic involvement, I participate in 30 to 50 different civic, professional, personal development, or spiritual organizations. I assess them each year based on my short-term and long-term goals in each area of my life. I determine whether they fit into the strategy and vision of my businesses and my personal or business goals. Then, I determine whether to give each my time, talent, or treasure. Sometimes it's one or the other, and other times, it's all three. After being involved on a national level with ten particular organizations over the last 40 years, I better understand that in the business community, we choose the organizations which best fit our profession. As a contractor in the construction industry since 1980, I participate in many associations that are related to my craft. As a result, I have decided to stay home some and create an association which would fit my needs for who and what I am.

- ✓ I am black.
- ✓ I am a woman.
- ✓ I am a general contractor.
- ✓ I am in the construction industry.
- ✓ I am interested in niched industries.

Being led by the Spirit, I created the National Association of Black Women in Construction (NABWIC), which is an organization comprised of all women focusing on Black women and girls in particular and all women and girls in the construction industry, in general. One purpose of the organization is to connect the millennials and the baby boomers, creating a pipeline that will make it easier for women in a male-dominated industry. Along with our team, we started the NABWIC Billionaire Dollar monthly luncheon, where each month, we invite owners of public agencies to share their master plan with us. The master plan or construction improvement projects (CIP) must include over a billion dollars in opportunities. For example, industries such as healthcare, transportation, energy, water utilities, ports, aviation, transient, facilities, housing, etc. This invitation draws architects, engineers and contractors to hear their owners describe upcoming opportunities, which is beneficial to the attendees. This effort allows our members to get to know, like, and begin to trust their clients in a social setting. The owners support us, as we help support them and their programs. Now I have a better understanding of what my father meant when he said, *"Ann, stay home some. Your friends can never come to your house because you are always at theirs."*

Building Networks

As a Rotarian, our motto is, "Service above Self." This statement is a reminder of why I serve in multiple civic organizations and associations. In every profession there are civic and professional organizations and associations that are operated and controlled by men who set policies which control that industry. These organizations go from general to specific. As a licensed general contractor that provides project control support in the transportation industry, we are involved with many of these professional organizations to help build our brand while building relationships in that niche. The Association of General Contractors (AGC) and the Association of Builders and Contractors (ABC) has chapters all over the United States. The ABC motto is, "If you are not in politics, you are not in business." This statement alone epitomizes the power an organization can have when it is politically minded in service. Any contractor, large or small would be wise to be connected to one or both of these organizations if they operate in the construction industry. Many minorities and/or women are normally small businesses. They must also be associated with a professional or civic organization that has a national presence in the industry. It does not matter what industry you are in, you must be involved in at least one organization connected to your industry. If you are a teacher, there are organizations for teachers. If you are a nurse, there are organizations for nurses, there are organizations for lawyers, doctors, engineers, media personalities, etc.

There is an organization connected to almost, if not all professions and you must be involved in at least one, especially one that is connected to what you do for a living and/or one that is connected to your passion, that thing you love. This is what I affectionately call "where the boys are". They control our industries, which covers our interests, which helps us to grow and to know what is happening on the national, state, and local levels. But in order to find out, you must participate and be a part of some of these organizations. You must network, get to know people, and learn the secrets that are not always known to the average person in the industry. In my opinion, "Where the boys are" refers to those who set policy and impact legislation to support their special interests. We become part of problem when we choose not to engage at any level, do the bare minimum and be mediocre while participating in nothing. Since 1990, MCO Construction has chosen to be involved with most major construction organizations at different levels. What we have learned from these relationships is the fact that people really do look to do business with those they know, like and trust, especially when it pertains to money.

Never too Young

"Civic education and civic responsibility should be taught in elementary school." (Donna Brazile) The quote from Ms. Brazile hit home for me in a very personal way. As I was reading the words of Ralph Waldo Emerson when he said, "Thoughts are the property of

those only who can entertain them." I had an aha moment because it provoked a thought I believed would change the history of a generation in construction by encouraging our youth to become more civic minded. As I entertained the thought, I decided to take our eight year-old granddaughter Rajah Nia Tate to the Congregational Black Caucus foundation convention in Washington, D.C. I believe it is never too soon to get her involved in civic engagement at a national level. It is critically important that she understands civic duties and gets involved civically early in life. While attending her first meeting with the National Association of Black Women in Construction, as everyone introduced themselves during the national strategic planning meeting, she introduced herself as the CEO of NABWIC. After the laughter subsided, the thought remained with me. Every civic movement starts with a thought, an idea, and the power to entertain that thought can be contagious. As I continued to think about my own civic ideas, such as creating a community of Black Women Contractors to encourage and support building a pipeline for the future, workforce, and entrepreneurs to be more civic-minded and give back, I realized that my ideas had become a reality. Civic education is vital, so much so, that the Congressional Black Caucus Foundation has created a leadership institute that prepares the next generation to take their places in the field of community service and policy development.

Simply having a thought to cross your mind, does not make it truly yours when it comes to civic involvement. You must actively consider, analyze, and grapple with the meaning of the thought, essentially acting on the thought. I am continually engaging and owning this idea of creating a more civic-minded group of young people in the construction industry. It is never too late to become civically informed and involved. Just ask congresswoman, Frederica S. Wilson as she acted upon the thought of 500 African American Role Models of Excellence which is now at 5,000 and counting. Act on your own thoughts and idea, believe that you can achieve them, and speak your own convictions while being civic-minded.

The Price we Pay

In good faith, you must always consider going the extra mile and rendering more and better service in and for your civic or professional organizations and also with everyone you come in contact with. This is because you will sooner or later receive compensation that exceeds the service you rendered. You will also have greater strength of character, and you will find it easier to go the extra mile each time. I call this working in a spirit of excellence. You will become known for quality, for integrity and for excellence. Working in a spirit of excellence does not require anyone's permission and it can be done when no one else is around. In fact, working in excellence when no one is looking is the true test of character.

By becoming known for excellence, you will create many opportunities which will surpass your wildest dreams, so if know that you don't work in excellence, start doing so. You can start by doing things without being asked. The law of increase and return states that what you get back will be greater than what you give. This law is operating all the time. And the return often comes in additional wages, promotion, and sometimes great peace of mind. So, when you give of your time, talents, and treasure to your civic or professional organizations, in time the law of increase and return shows up often, when you least expect it.

We often hear that service is the price we pay for the space we occupy. Scripture says, *"Do unto others as you would have them do unto you?"* We do that through service to others. Start the habit of doing more than you are paid for and watch what happens. Eventually you will be paid for more than you do. As you continue to a life of significance through service, you leave your legacy that will continue to reverberate in the earth when you are long gone. You may be gone, but your thoughts, ideas and advice to others still lives on. Truly living a successful life is a gradual process. It must begin with service. It can begin in no other way. If we really want money, we must first serve. Look at the lives of truly successful people. In the long term, they are the ones who give real service.

William Blakely, the great theologian quoted, *"Give without remembering, and receive without forgetting."* Once you have exerted your passion and goals into a particular industry, consider getting involved in the civic, professional, or philanthropic association or organization associated with that industry. Then serve. Decide whether you are going to give your time, talent, or treasure without expecting anything in return. Give one, two or all three. Also be able to determine *why* you are giving. Is it for your own personal growth and development or is it for social causes? Does your job require it of you, or are you doing it on your own to expand your knowledge of the field? You must know the answer to the question of why you are serving? Once you decide whether to give of your time, talent, or treasure, then everything all goes back to money. You may want to give of your time, but find that if you give too much time, you are unable to make money. There also needs to be balance between your family, your profession, your business and the organizations to which you belong. Striking a balance is the key. I am learning that many people looking for meaning and significance in life, find it by losing themselves in causes greater than themselves.

When you find a civic organization or association, you may find new opportunities to find new money. Surveys have shown that a small percentage of professionals belong to organizations beyond their profession, and many are in unproductive organizations or associations. You must be in an organization that is adding value to you as a person. If you are not a member of any civic organization, then now is a good time to research the best one for you and, then select one and become a member. Then, join a committee to volunteer your time, talents, and treasures to help the organization grow. You may be thinking, *I just don't have the time.* What you are really saying is that there are other things more important to you, so what is the truth about it, because we all have the same 24 hours in a day. No-one has more than anyone else.

The point here is that sometimes we do not place the same level of importance on those things that are truly important. We tend to give the most amount of time to the things that do not matter much. We major in the minors and minor in the majors. You would be surprised to discover just how much of your time goes here and there when you could be using it to do something productive. You have time to do everything else that you want to do, but no time to join an organization that could potentially be a great benefit to you?

Your Core Mission in Life

I wholeheartedly believe this statement: "Service is the price we pay for the space we occupy." But is service a price or an investment? Let's analyze. If service is an investment, then how do you determine where you serve? What is your service? How long will you serve in a particular capacity? Service is rendered by giving. The giving of time, talent, and treasure to worthy causes. Through service, we must learn to use the winds of adversity to steer that ship called life. The habit of rendering more and better service than you are paid for at all times with a pleasant and pleasing attitude, and by going the extra mile, will give you greater opportunities in business and the civic area of your life. This is a natural law of giving and receiving. You can't render a great service today, then, expect a return on your investment tomorrow. Things take time.

When a gardener plants a seed in the ground, he or she does not instantly see a result. A plant is not even seen after a few days or a few weeks, but that does not mean that there is no seed there. The gardener is not concerned that he or she cannot see a plant yet. They have faith that the seed is there and so they water that area, cultivate that area, and make sure that the place where the seed is planted has plenty of sunshine and air. Eventually, something begins to appear in the very spot where the seed was planted. As the plant begins to burst forth out of the ground, the gardener continues to cultivate, water, and nurture until the plant is fully visible and eventually healthy and strong. Initially, there was no indication in the natural realm that a plant even existed where the seed was sown, but there were powerful forces at work underneath the surface. As the manifestation appeared, it was evident that the one seed, in the process of growing, multiplied, proving that inherent in the law of growth, there is a law of multiplicity. It also proves that you not only reap what you sow, but you get a surplus (or double for the trouble) for the time, effort, and sacrifice that was put into sowing, cultivating, nurturing, and watering the seed. This is how it works with service. Continue to render more service that what you are getting.

Continue working in a spirit of excellence, going over and beyond, doing things that are not asked of you and being pleasant, kind, and courteous while doing all of this. When you least expect it, you will be able to look around at the beautiful harvest that has sprung up. This could be a harvest of financial blessings, beautiful surroundings, a home filled with love and laughter, or simple peace and contentment. In due season, you will reap what you have planted according to the nature of the seed. You must therefore be sure before you plant a seed (your service) that you are going to be satisfied with the harvest you are going to get in return. Helping others unlocks cells within your brain which gives you the answers to your problems. This is the foundation upon which many civic organizations have been built.

The more I live, I strive to do more each day to help others rise because we can all win as we learn how to connect our civic involvement to our personal dreams. It is the dreamer who sees the interconnectedness of the human causes that gives birth to civic organizations. It is these dreamers who begin to see that their contributions help to build a better world. George Bernard Shaw, the great English playwriter put it this way, *"I am convinced that my life belongs to the whole community, and as long as I live, it is my privilege to do for it whatever I can. The harder I work, the more I live. I rejoice in life for its own sake. Life is no brief candle for me. It is a source of splendid torch which I got to hold for a brief moment, and I want to make it burn as brightly as I possibly can before turning it over to the next generation."*

BUILDERS TOOLBOX 

- ❖ How does participation in industry-specific organizations help build relationships and knowledge within your field?

- ❖ How can joining civic and professional organizations impact your community involvement and career?

- ❖ Why is it important to understand how the government functions at local, state, and national levels?

- ❖ What role does voting and staying informed about current events play in your life?

- ❖ How did Ann McNeill's childhood experiences influence her civic involvement and professional success?

You Must have a Dream!

What is your dream in the area of your Civics?
Write it down.

9
Recreation

I like to take walks in the park by myself when no one can bother me and I can think.
~Magic Johnson

You must have a dream to have a dream come true in the recreation area of your life. This allows you to recreate. All work and no play, makes Jack a dull boy. This is an old adage, but a true one. Without relaxation, Jack is headed towards a breakdown. Recreation serves as a refreshing break from daily routines because it strikes a balance between work and play. Without recreation, one will not experience true fulfillment in life. Recreation is any activity that you do for enjoyment, relaxation, or pleasure, providing a break from routines and responsibilities. For those of us with busy lives, such as business owners, parents, or employees, recreation is essential for maintaining mental health and achieving balance. Examples of recreational activities include traveling, walking, jogging, swimming, playing sports, line dancing or regular dancing, going to concerts, movies, restaurants, engaging in hobbies, indoor games, outdoor games, or spending quality time with family and friends.

Maintaining recreational balance should be a priority in everyone's life. The benefits of recreation can significantly reduce stress, improve your mood, and enhance your overall well-being. Recreation is a balance between the demands of work and personal responsibilities offering an outlet for relaxation and mental rejuvenation. For someone who has a hectic schedule, making time for recreational activities is extremely important. One of the most stressful jobs there is, is that of being the president of the United States, but even they take time to release stress. We see them playing golf and participating in fun events at times. Surely, your life is not as stressful as that of the Commander in Chief. Fitting recreation into your schedule requires intentional planning and prioritization, but the benefits that it offers in terms of stress relief, mental clarity, and improved quality of life make recreation a great investment. Set recreational goals in advance. For where do you desire to travel? Do you have a recreational bucket list? Early in my childhood, I loved to travel. Every summer, my parents would travel from Florida to Cordele, Georgia to visit relatives and friends. When I returned from summer vacation, the teachers would ask every student to share what they did during their summer vacation. As students, we enjoyed sharing and hearing the travel stories and journeys of our friends. I believed that my imagination at a very early age became heighted to travel to more adventurous places and to continue to share my journey to encourage and inspire others to travel more as well.

As I grew older, the desire to travel farther and to see more of the world, grew stronger. I began to associate travel with recreation, fun, and growth. As I entered college at Florida Memorial University, my freshman workstudy teacher Ms. Trudy Hoo, encouraged me to volunteer and to travel internationally with her science club. To afford the trips, we sold doughnuts and coffee every morning to raise the funds. After graduation, this desire continued to grow. As of this writing (January, 2025), I have traveled to over 30 countries and growing.

Take Time for Breaks

Recreation is essential for maintaining both physical and mental well-being, as it acts as a crucial counterbalance to the pressure of life. At the start of August 2024, I committed to visiting a new park or museum every day. Why this goal? In my Clarity Mastermind Group, for the month of August, we emphasized the importance of recreational goals and taking time for breaks, so on the very first day, I discovered four parks within walking distance of my office, providing a perfect escape from the usual stress and a chance to unwind, rejuvenate and refresh daily. After discovering this park, I discovered 20 new parks and now this is something I look forward to when I travel. My favorite park was Centennial Olympica Park in Atlanta, GA. Actively pursuing this particular recreational goal, has sparked my creativity and it also promotes a healthier lifestyle through physical activity. It supports cognitive and emotional development by offering chances to sit in solitude as I am reading and listening to nature. By making recreation a priority in your life, you enhance your overall quality of life, which in turn boosts your productivity and cognition in other areas. This is why I like the following quote by Magic Johnson: *A daily walk is my recreation of choice. Oftentimes, I will walk and talk or walk and listen to audio recordings or just walk in silence. Your mind, body, and spirit need a refreshing break at times. When your mind is packed with so many things, it needs an outlet that is free from stress. When a tired body and a tired mind need to relax, recreational activities come to the rescue. It is necessary take a break from the mental and physical realities of the daily grind. A benefit of recreational activities is that they rejuvenate and energize the mind and body and prepares you to better face challenges of life. Recreation is also an excellent way to renew your interests. It is a way to not get bored, fatigued, stressed, or frustrated and start really living.*

Promises to Keep

One of the things that I delight myself in, is that I work towards always keeping my word. One family recreational goal was to go to Disney every year when the children were smaller. A promise made should be a promise kept. As busy as I am, I always made time for my grandson. One particular year, I had promised to take my grandson Malachi and his friend Stephan, who were both eight at the time, to Disney World when they were nine years old. The promise was made at the beginning of the year, but as the summer came and was quickly leaving, I had not yet taken them. We had set the date and as fate would have it, many challenges arose. At the time that we were supposed to go, I was super busy, and work dictated that I attend to the needs of my clients, but I knew I had to keep my promise to them, so I dropped everything and we set off for Orlando late that evening in the storming rain. I had not confirmed a reservation at any hotel, so we did not have a place to stay, but by faith, I knew we would find some place to stay. As I was driving, the bottom fell out of the sky and it rained for hours, but I had a personal decision to make. Do I keep the promise to the children and continue driving in such bad weather or do I turn around and go back home for safety reasons? If they were adults, they would understand, but if I did not take them, my promise would have been broken forever.

As children, all they would have remembered is that I did not keep my promise to them. Considering everything, I decided to collect the boys, get on the road, and head to Orlando. We packed the car and I drove very slowly all the way there. We pressed our way, found a hotel, checked in and had dinner. The following morning, as the sun came up in Orlando, it was a beautiful day for Disney. The boys ran around, laughed, got on rides, and were so happy. They had a wonderful time in Orlando, and I did not regret the recreational goal and keeping my promise to them. I watched the two of them float in the lazy river pool. That weekend get-away was also good for me because it provided a brief outlet for relaxing, temporarily diverting my attention away from clients and work and focusing on my grandson and his friend while also taking time for myself to relax. As of this writing (2024), they are now both over 25 years old and they still talk about the fun they had each year when I took them to Disney as children. A promise kept is more important than a promise made, but not kept. These are also recreational memories that I will always remember.

If you can Dream it, you can do it!

Traveling to Africa was another recreational goal that I had for years. I had always dreamed of going to Africa, and everyone who knew me, knew about my dream because I made it known to them all. Every time I spoke of my desire to travel to Africa, I strengthened the conviction within me and allowed my words to search for the elements that would make it possible for me to go. Then, the opportunity finally came. I could not afford it, but when there is a strong will, a way will be found. My friend William S. Stevens, called to tell me that he had read an article in a magazine that the Congress of Black Mayors was planning a conference in Africa. He suggested that I call the tour guide and to see if I could go on the group rate. Perhaps they would let me tag along. The worse thing that could happen is that they would say no. When I called, they obliged me and allowed me to go on the group rate, but the deadline had passed, so they gave me one day to get the $1,200 payment to them.

When I got home, I shared the opportunity with my husband, who had heard me speak for years about wanting to travel to Africa. He heard the excitement in my voice and saw it on my face, so he did not hesitate to support me. This was the trip of a lifetime for me! This situation demonstrated that when you have a desire, a dream, or an aspiration, never let it die. Keep speaking about it, thinking about it, and keep it at the forefront of your mind. An opportunity will eventually come for you to bring that desire into fruition. I traveled to African and visited Ivory Coast, Senegal, and Liberia. You must jump on the opportunity when it presents itself or it will pass you by! This was another recreational dream that came true!

Exposure is Priceless!

Traveling to Africa was a dream come true for me. Many years after that trip, I had the deep desire to share the dream of Africa with my daughter, but again, I couldn't afford it. However, my dream to go again, was bigger than my inability to afford it. Even though I did not have the money, I refused to let the $2,000 cost of the trip hinder us from going. Dr. Leon Sullivan, a Baptist Minister and renown civil rights leader had planned, what he called, the African American experience, consisting of two chartered planes that took Blacks to Africa to meet Africans. He did this every two years. Knowing this, I would send $25 money orders every week to pay for the trip, so when it was time to go, I took my then six-year-old daughter Ionnie with me. When we landed, the African dancers came up to plane's door and serenaded everyone on the flight.

Ionnie began to cry while tugging at me. She shared how embarrassed she was once she saw the beautiful African dancers. She told me that she felt bad because she thought that all Africans were like the people she had seen on the Tarzan movies on TV, a White man running around chasing Africans. That was her perception of Africans and sadly demonstrates the impact of negative TV programing. It is amazing how we do not know what is going on in the minds of our children, especially when they are not exposed to different things, so what they see on TV is what they think is reality. We do not know how they perceive the world until they are exposed to different cultures, places, and people. This is why recreation, exposure, and healthy communication with them is important. I thought to myself that all the sacrifices I made to make the trip possible to take her was well worth it. From a recreational standpoint, we must expose our children to more. This expands their creativity and how they see themselves in the world.

This is Living Grandma!

It was the summer of 2006, when I hosted my annual company retreat for my MCO Construction employees at the Sonesta Beach Hotel at Key Biscayne in Miami. We rented a three-bedroom suite, and I brought my entire staff. I also bought Stephan and Malachi with me. The boys played, ate, swam in the hotel's pool, and vacationed for an entire week while I did retreat activities with my staff. The following week, we went to the National Speakers Association (NSA) Conference in Orlando and stayed at the Marriott Hotel. Again, the boys played, ate, and swam. The next week, we went to another conference and stayed at another five-star World Marriott in Orlando. When Malachi walked in, he looked around at the marble floors, the décor, the pool, the ambiance and turned to me and said, *"Now this is living Grandma!"* He had not seen anything so luxurious before. On the journey of exposing our children to various experiences, we must consider what they will see, hear, and feel how it will affect and shape them.

When children see more, it expands their minds to what they can accomplish and what they could possibly have later in life. Making sacrifices and exposing our children and grandchildren to the finer things in life, in spite of our financial situation, has enabled them to see and experience different cultures, customs, and in turn, has taught them to appreciate much of what this world has to offer. Family is a precious gift and when we strategically treat that gift with value, we will begin to see that value expand. Invest in your family and watch the returns on your investments multiply!

Recreation not only offers immediate benefits for mental health and overall well-being, but it also creates lasting memories that will be cherished for a lifetime. These moments, often captured in pictures, remind us of the joy, laughter, and fun experienced. If we spend our lives solely focused on work, without making time for recreational activities, we risk letting life pass us by, filled with regrets for not seizing moments of happiness and exposure to new experiences. To truly live a fulfilling life, it is essential to "make" time for recreation. Prioritize activities that bring joy and relaxation into your busy schedule. You will not regret it. The memories and benefits of recreation are invaluable, enriching your life in ways that work alone cannot provide.

 **BUILDERS TOOLBOX**

❖ Why is recreation essential for maintaining mental health and achieving balance in life?

❖ How did Ann McNeill's experiences with her grandson demonstrate the importance of keeping promises related to recreational activities?

❖ What impact did Ann McNeill's trip to Africa have on her and her daughter's perceptions and understanding of different cultures?

❖ How can exposure to diverse recreational experiences expand a child's mind and influence their future aspirations?

❖ How can making time for recreation prevent a life filled with regrets and missed opportunities for joy and relaxation?

You Must have a Dream!

What is your dream in the area of your
Recreation? Write it down.

10

Creativity

*When we move toward our own creativity, we move towards
our Creator.*
~Julia Cameron

You must have a dream to have a dream come true in the area of creativity, so what are you creating? Are you stuck? Do you journal? In 1994, I began the active path to search for a process, a method, a framework to learn how to journal my thoughts. I did not realize that at this particular time, the journey of journaling and connecting to the Creator would lead me to creating so many new things; nor did I realize the road of 1,000 days of journaling started with one day, then another, then another. Scholar and poet Jalal Al-din quoted the following saying which resonates deeply with me; *"What you seek, is seeking you."* The book, 'The Artist Way' was seeking me as I was seeking a process to learn how to journal. The Artist Way by Julian Cameron showed up in my life in one week, three times on three different days. On the 4th day, my friend Beatrice Louissaint, President/CEO of Florida State Minority Supplier Development Council, called me from the bookstore and said these words, *"Hi Ann. I am here at Barnes and Noble. I know you love to read. What are two books you want, and I will bring them by?"* I said, 'The Artist Way' and the Four Hour Workweek. Within the hour, she brought the books to my home. That same night, I began to read 'The Artist Way.' The following morning, I started to practice her bedrock tool for creative recovery, which is a daily practice called "morning pages" which is three pages of longhand stream of conscious writing done first thing in the morning. Throught this process, you are writing anything and everything on the page.

What Exactly is Creativity?

Some people think that creativity is only generating an idea and others think that it is producing artwork. Still, others believe that creativity is coming up with something unique. During my research, the definition I like best is the following: "Creativity is producing a new idea which adds value to someone." This to me, is creativity. I find that it is easy to generate ideas, but the challenge is the fact that the execution of the idea requires more creative action to implement said idea. Emerson said, *"Thoughts are the property of those who can entertain them because once you have the thought, you must be willing to engage it, to entertain it, and have the capacity to analyze it."* This quote reminds me of the actions that are required to execute your creative ideas with a process. My idea process for cultivating creativity starts with my struggles, problems and challenges. I believe the process of inspiring your creativity may start with you defining your struggles, problems and challenges as well. This is the first step. For example, early in my career, I was financially destitute, but I had a desire to make money – lots of money and eventually become financially free. This desire led me to the book, 'Think and Grow Rich.' The principles from the book sparked creative ideas in me. The new ideas compelled me to action and the actions required me to grow. The book also challenged me to identify individuals who had the same financial problems I had. Doing this, inspired me to help others with their financial problems, which in turn, helped me with mine. Over the years, I am learning that there are three elements or activities that oftentimes inspire my creativity. As a result, I have been able to produce and implement new and inspiring ideas that have emerged out of tapping into my creative faculty.

This process for me is also about understanding and absorbing knowledge and insights around the problem that I am facing and defining the constraints of which I must overcome. I am also learning that ideas just don't arrive. They are built on the knowledge that you already have with insights that create new connections in the brain. For example, I read a story in the book, 'Think and Grow Rich' about the formation of U.S. Steel Corporation. While reading the story year after year after year, the connections in my brain began to form a creative idea to help me with the financial problem that I had of covering my construction company's payroll.

The second step of creating an idea is incubation which should lead to maturation. In the above-mentioned story about the U.S. Steel Corporation, Charles Schwab had a billion dollar idea to create U.S. Steel by delivering a billion dollar dinner speech. As I repeatedly read this story year after year, an idea of creating a billion dollar luncheon event within the National Association of Black Women in Construction (NABWIC) emerged. This is only one example of the incubation that led to maturation (the first step). We all have ideas but they are sometimes stillborn until we bring them to maturation or full term to see the light of day. Many ideas happen when you prepare your brain with the knowledge and insights, then step away and give them time to mature. Always remember to return and complete the process of bringing your idea to fruition.

In my construction company, finding ways to make payroll in the face of financial challenges, was another example of maturation. This period included but was not limited to calling friends and family on a weekly basis, calling banks and liquor stores to borrow money, getting payday loans, maxing out credit cards and retirement accounts, borrowing money through receivable financing as I continuously asked for help. Since 1982, which was the start of my construction company, I have never missed making payroll to my employees. During this maturation, I learned to give respect to all creative ideas and to act on them, especially those that seem strange or absurd. Always be willing by faith to be optimistically objective with your creative ideas. Here it is years later, I am able to teach and consult others on finding ways to tap into creativity, which will produce opportunities in the construction industry by tapping into wisdom, knowledge and understanding of what's possible when you have faith and belief. It is possible to create, so move your feet to match your faith and create.

Creativity is the ability to generate new and original ideas, solutions, or approaches by thinking outside the box. Embracing creativity in your life means being open to new experiences, experimenting with different perspectives, and continuously learning. Cultivating creativity can be achieved by exploring your curiosity, practicing mindfulness, engaging in new and different activities, and allowing yourself to take risks and make mistakes. Creativity in your life can be nurtured through activities such as reading, exploring new hobbies, and allowing time for reflection and brainstorming. In your personal life, creativity can enhance problem-solving skills, enrich your personal relationships, and improve your overall well-being by offering fresh perspectives and solutions. It is creativity that drives innovation in businesses and organizations because creativity helps to develop unique products or services and improves efficiency. For instance, a business owner who embraces creativity can stand out in a crowded market by offering distinctive and appealing solutions to customers. You can also have a dream in the area of creativity.

Benefits of Being Creative

Creativity isn't just about art. It's about thinking differently, solving problems, and bringing fresh perspectives to every aspect of your life. Whether you are looking to innovate in your career, enrich your personal relationships, or simply explore new hobbies, creativity is the key to unlocking endless possibilities. Being creative sets you apart and gives you a distinct identity that can lead to recognition and success. When you are a person who is known for thinking outside of the box in a positive way, people think of you when they need something unique that you can offer. For business owners, creativity translates to a competitive advantage that attracts customers who seek innovative and differentiated offerings. All of us have specific skills, but those who apply creativity to their skills allow for the development of strategic approaches that distinguishes them from others with similar skills.

Setting Yourself Apart Creatively

I am inspired by the quote from Dr. Martin Luther King, "I have a dream!" This quote allows me to be free to create, to set myself apart. One of the ways I do that is by rising early and planning while setting goals to achieve my dreams. This quiet time allows me to reflect and embrace the disciplines that are necessary to write daily. These daily disciplines would also allow you to review the end of the week to see the benefits of embracing a process. It also allows you to reflect on the doors that have opened and take moments to reflect on the changes required for you to make adjustments in future actions. Reflecting gives you a clear vision to identify any possibilities that may have been missed from the previous day and to embrace opportunities which may emerge. This time of reflection brings you closer to your dreams. This self-improvement is about learning new things through reflection while on the path of life. This is setting yourself apart creatively.

Creativity enables you to stand out. Setting yourself apart through creativity involves leveraging your unique perspectives and talents in a way that sheds light on your originality. This could be through personal projects, hobbies, or contributions to your community that reflect your innovative thinking. When you embrace the art of being creative, it enriches all aspects of life, from personal growth to professional success. It is essential to work at embracing creativity in order to unlock its many benefits. Cultivating creativity can be achieved by fostering curiosity, practicing mindfulness, engaging in activities that you never would have gravitated to, and allowing oneself to take risks and make mistakes.

Cultivating Creativity

Curiosity drives your desire to learn and explore. Staying curious involves constantly seeking new knowledge, asking questions, and being open to discovering new ideas in the silence. "That path of things is silence" (Ralph Waldo Emerson). This mindset encourages continuous growth and prevents you from becoming stagnant. By asking questions, you are challenging assumptions and deepening your understanding of different subjects, which can lead to more ideas and solutions. Embracing curiosity means seeing the world with a sense of wonder and always looking for ways to expand your horizons.

Cultivating creativity is also developed by studying to be silent. In the book of 1 Thessalonians 4:11, it states to, "Study to be silent and do your own business and work with your own hands." Creatively, do you study to be silent? Over the years, as I cultivate creativity, I've created a process called, "My daily date with myself." My morning routine for my daily date with myself journey includes, but is not limited to the following:

1. Rise daily between 3:00-5:00a.m.
2. Pray and meditate
3. Write two-three things down that I am grateful for
4. Sitting for ideas process
5. Watch and exercise from a five-minute yoga video while listening to Tasha Cobb on my headphones
6. Journal my thoughts
7. Read two-three pages from two-three books
8. Drink 20-30 ounces of water
9. Drink a vitamin mix
10. Walk for 30 minutes to an hour
11. Eat fruit and nuts while walking
12. Listen to a TEDx video on one of the ten areas of my life
13. Read, write and post my utmost prayer meditation
14. Listen to a YouTube Proverb for the day by David Suchet
15. Listen to five-ten minutes of Myron Golden
16. Write ten opportunities every day in my journal
17. Prepare for work

Being Present and Aware

Mindfulness is the practice of being fully focused on the current moment. It involves paying attention to your thoughts, feelings, and surroundings. The process of being present and aware is helping me to become more insightful, as I understand the value of making application of the knowledge which I am gaining, especially in the silence. Dr. Myles Munroe reminded us that our purpose is not found in the noise, it is found in the quiet. I believe our creativity is also heightened in the silence while being present and aware. When you practice mindfulness, it enhances creativity by helping you become more aware of your experiences and reactions and allows you to respond to situations with clarity and insight. This heightened awareness can lead to more thoughtful and innovative approaches to problems and opportunities, fostering a deeper connection to your creative process. Engaging in diverse activities opens your perspectives and exposes you to new experiences. Stepping outside your comfort zone allows you to experience different cultures, ideas, and practices, which can inspire creativity. Trying new hobbies, traveling, or learning new skills can provide fresh insights and stimulate your imagination. By diversifying your experiences, you are able to open your mind to new and fresh ideas that you never had thought of or considered before. As an adult, I am just becoming aware of the true impact of watching my mother as a young child, practice what I now understand as the benefit of the silence. Every morning when I woke up, I found her sitting quietly with her Bible in her lap; and the older I get, the more aware I am becoming as I practice the same. I am encouraged by Rick Warren's quote which helps me to see how my creativity continues to connect me to my purpose; "Purpose is about living for the one who created me and chasing the call of my life is found in the silence.

Risk-Taking

Risk-taking is essential for creativity because it involves stepping into the unknown and experimenting with new ideas. Allowing yourself to fail means embracing the possibility of making mistakes, then learning from them and using them as valuable learning opportunities. Each failure provides insights that can help you to readjust your approach, leading to success in the future. By adopting a growth mindset and viewing your failures as steppingstones rather than setbacks, you strengthen your resilience and build the courage to take bold, creative risks that can result in a taking your life to a whole new level.

In your personal life, creativity can bring unique ways of solving problems and can assist you in decision-making by guiding you towards decisions that have an element of ingenuity within them. In work life, creativity enhances productivity and job satisfaction. It empowers you to approach tasks and projects with fresh perspectives and assists in finding more efficient and effective ways to achieve your goals and meet your deadlines. Bringing creativity into your work promotes a collaborative team environment, where innovative ideas are encouraged and valued. This not only boosts morale but also drives organizational growth. Embracing creativity in your professional life ensures that you remain adaptable and valuable in a rapidly changing work landscape.

Personal Branding

Personal branding means standing out in a competitive landscape. By building a strong personal brand, you create a distinctive identity that reflects your values, expertise, and personality. This involves consistently presenting yourself in a way that highlights your strengths and differentiates you from others. My advice is to utilize various platforms such as social media, your personal website, and professional networks to share your creative work, ideas, and achievements. Effective personal branding can lead to new opportunities, professional growth, and recognition, making you a sought-after individual in your field.

Creative networking involves seeking out and participating in unique opportunities to connect with others. This may include attending industry conferences, joining online communities, participating in workshops, and engaging in social events. By approaching networking with creativity, you can build meaningful relationships that go beyond traditional interactions. When you collaborate on projects, share ideas, and support the growth of those you network with, you strengthen your social capital, expand your connections and in many cases, forge new friendships. Creative networking opens doors to diverse perspectives, new insights, and potential partnerships. Being creative while networking helps you to build a robust professional network that can provide support, inspiration, and opportunities for collaboration, while enhancing both your personal and professional life.

In chapter four, we talked about lifelong learning, which is the continuous pursuit of knowledge and skills throughout your life. Embracing lifelong learning with a focus on being creative while acquiring knowledge means constantly seeking out new methods, techniques, and perspectives to enhance your capabilities. This can involve taking courses, reading extensively, attending workshops, and experimenting with new ideas. By remaining curious and open to new experiences, you can stay ahead of industry trends, improve your problem-solving abilities, and innovate in your personal and professional life. Lifelong learning ensures that you remain adaptable, relevant, and capable of navigating changes while contributing creatively to your field.

Curiosity

Curiosity is not a trait to avoid. It drives your desire to learn and explore. Being curious does not mean being nosy. It means asking questions, constantly seeking new knowledge, and being open to discovering new ideas. This curious, yet creative mindset encourages continuous growth and prevents stagnation. By asking questions, you challenge assumptions and deepen your understanding of various subjects, which can lead to innovative ideas and solutions. Embracing curiosity means seeing the world with a sense of wonder and always looking for ways to expand your horizons.

BUILDERS TOOLBOX 

* Why is meditation important for enhancing creativity, and how can you practice it?

* What are the benefits of engaging in new and diverse activities for your creative process?

* How does taking risks contribute to developing creativity, and how can you overcome the fear of failure?

* How can you set yourself apart creatively in your personal and professional life?

* How can you effectively build your personal brand?

* Why is lifelong learning essential for maintaining and enhancing creativity, and how can you incorporate it into your routine?

There was a time in my business career that I owed the IRS substantially, and with penalties and interest, the bill had gotten up to $500,000! Yes, I owed the IRS half a million dollars!

You Must have a Dream!

What is your dream in the area of your
Creativity? Write it down.

Epilogue

"I have a dream"
~Dr. Martin Luther King

By this point in the book, you have learned just a little about my journey and some of the lessons that I have gleaned along the way as entrepreneur and founder of many businesses. You have read some of the chapters devoted to developing dreams in every area of my life. My desire for you is to develop and/or create dreams for yourself in every area of your life. I hope you have learned some things you could do to reach your goals and also some things to avoid from some of the setbacks that I have experienced.

On the journey of pursuing my desire, life happened; and it is still happening all along the way. While writing this book and reflection on the dreams s in every area of my life, I am realizing that on Dec. 31, 1979 when I decided that I did not want to continue to live the aimless life that I was living up to that point, I began to dream about what my life would look like in my 30s, 40s 50s up to 100 years old. But at this writing, I have celebrated my 70th birthday and many of the dreams that I wrote in each area of my life is still manifesting. Largely because I created a framework, a process, an assessment for every area of my life. That assessment is now called the McNeill Factor Self-Assessment Survey. This survey you where you are right now and where you want to be in the ten areas of your life. These areas include (but does not have to be limited to) spiritual, family, financial, education, health, personal development, business/career, recreation, civic, creativity. It shows you areas where you are strong or weak or need improvement. Over the years, my clients have been able to determine where they need to improve. As the years have passed, I have read hundreds of books from the world's greatest thinkers. Many books are personal development which include the ten categories of my life. As I began to digest the information connecting the dots of the insights, the wisdom, the knowledge and the understanding of many structures, models and frameworks. It is becoming clearer to me that all principles are built upon the Bible and with that knowledge, I am exactly where I need to be, learning to overcome every struggle, every challenge and every problem, as I am becoming who God has predestined me to be, but I must continue to do the inner work. This is the work that precedes the "be" "do" "have". I am also learning that we cannot express powers which we do not possess. Charles Haanel's quote helps me to understand clearly, "We must "be" before we can "do" and we can "do" only to the extent to which we "are" and so what we do will coincide with what we "are" and what we "are" depends upon what we "think."

I began to develop my own success model that works for me and my clients. This book is just the beginning of that journey. This journey includes new beliefs and new philosophies that are integrated into your life. It all starts with your dreams and your desires for a better quality of life in every area of your life with accountability. This process allows you to create from a different set of beliefs and values. For example, you too can begin to institute a daily date with yourself, which includes a time of reflection, meditation, affirmations, prayers, and journaling. This would enhance your quality of life. This process supports strengthening your confidence and your beliefs. As we change our beliefs, everything else changes. Learning from this process allows you to change your mind and your body with the principles of autosuggestion and affirmations. This process can support healing and growth in every area. Over the years, I have enrolled in many self-help programs and invested thousands of dollars in my own personal development. But all in all, I could not find a program that helped me to create and achieve my dreams in every area of my life, especially in my businesses, so I created this one for myself after many years of searching. Eventually, others started asking if I can share, teach, coach, or consult with them so they too can have similar results. This required me to continue to define and refine the framework into a systematized documented process. We are all looking for transformation and the benefits derived from the achievements of having our dreams come true, but are we all willing to do the work on the journey? This book, program and my proven process may not be for everyone. This is a journey, not a destination because we and our dreams are forever evolving.

Ann McNeill

Ann McNeill is President/CEO of one of South Florida's few African American-female owned construction companies. McNeill Construction (MCO) was founded 40 years ago and is still one of the leading minority firms in South Florida in the area of construction management and project controls. MCO construction has worked on the majority of the flagship projects in South Florida, such as The Miami Airlines Arena, The Marlins Ballpark, The Miami International Airport, The Miami Science Museum, The Miami Children's Courthouse and many more.

As a female licensed general contractor, Ann discovered that women in the construction business were far and few between. She strongly believed that a network of women in construction needed to be created. As a result, Ann started The National Association of Black Women in Construction (NABWIC). The association was created to help build a pipeline for black women in the public sector, black women in the private sector, Black women entrepreneurs, and young ladies in school. The main purpose of NABWIC is to create a network of professional women in the construction industry who teach each other how to turn contacts into contracts. This is done through a "Billion Dollar Luncheon", which is held each month. As a result of her track record of accomplishments, Ann has been featured in Black Enterprise Magazine, USA Today and ABC's World News.

She is also President of MCO Consulting, Inc., a consulting company that provides outreach, monitoring and compliance for private sector firms that work on public sector land. She has received numerous awards and recognitions for her work in her industry and also in the community. She received her Bachelor's Degree in accounting from Florida Memorial College (University) and her Master's Degree in finance from Barry University. She is married to Daniel McNeill and has two daughters, Danelle and Ionnie. She also has one grandson, Malachi and a granddaughter, Rajahnia.

Other Books by Ann McNeill

You Must have a Dream to have a Dream Come True! (The Workbook)
How to Raise a baby Billionaire
No Glory Without Story Stepping out on Faith to Birth the Business within You! (an anthology)
How to Start and run a Mastermind Group
How to Start and run a Mastermind Group (Workbook)
This is Living (A Journal)
My Daily Date with myself (A Journal)
Remember me this Way (A Workbook)

Recommended Readings by Ann McNeill

The Bible
Think and Grow Rich by Napolean Hill
Conscious Language
The E-Myth revisited by Michael Gerber
Fit for Life by Harvey and Marilyn Diamond
How I raised myself from Failure to Success Through Selling by Frank Bettger
Prosperity is your birthright by Dr. Mia Y. Merritt
Success, the Glenn Bland Method by Glenn Bland
The Artist Way by Julia Cameron
The Automatic Millionaire by David Bach
The Master Key System by Charless Haanel
The Subconscious Mind by Joseph Murphey